Acknowledgements

Thanks to Ed Lacey
for supplying the photographs

DORIAN WILLIAMS' WORLD OF SHOWJUMPING

FOREWORD

Sport holds a remarkable place in the affections of the British people. For some it is an active pursuit from which they obtain great personal satisfaction. For others it is the glamour of the big occasion or the reflected glory of the achievements of fellow countrymen throughout the world. For all of us, I suspect, there is a nostalgia based upon the doings of our great heroes and the sense of occasion in which we participated just because 'we were there' or, more often the case now, 'we saw it as it happened'.

Whether we were there, or whether we were viewing, there is no doubt that the written word is still the best means of widening our thinking and our appreciation of the subject. It seems remarkable to me that the development of sports literature has not kept pace with the development of sport itself.

The need for a good sports library, reasonably priced, easy to read for the ordinary sports fan, full of topical thinking and at the same time a handy reference to the year's events, was an obvious requirement for sport. I believe that the 'World of Sport' library matches that need for the first time and brings the ownership of a personal sports library within the reach of everyone. The Editorial Board and the authors hope that you will find the current series as enjoyable and interesting to read, and to possess, as we have done in producing them.

DENIS HOWELL, M.P.

SBN 361 01766 9
© 1971 Bagenal Harvey Organisation
Published in 1971 by Purnell, London.
Printed in Italy by Interlitho SPA

DORIAN WILLIAMS' WORLD OF SHOWJUMPING

Reporter:

Michael Clayton

EDITOR-IN-CHIEF   DENIS HOWELL, M.P.

PURNELL
London

CONTENTS

INTRODUCTION

Never has British show jumping achieved so much; never before has the overseas challenge been so formidable.

All this makes the world of Dorian Williams more fascinating than ever. The thousands who ride and attend shows regularly, the many millions who simply watch show jumping on television, will find international competition becoming even tougher and more exciting in the months ahead.

For this reason we look towards Britain's prospects in the Olympic Games at Munich, as well as charting the rising success of some new British show jumping stars.

The health of show jumping at the top depends on the growth of the sport among the lower grades where novice horses and riders gain vital experience. We look at some new trends expected in the 'seventies as many British horse shows suffer from an economic frost.

One of the joys of collaborating on this book with Dorian Williams is his many-sided interest in the horse world. Millions know him best for his commentaries at the Royal International Horse Show and the Horse of the Year Show; this year he was also commentating at some major events at the famous Sussex course at Hickstead, and we explore Hickstead's fascinating past and future.

Yet Dorian's interest and participation extends from show jumping to horse trials, dressage, showing and the hunting field. He makes a major contribution to these sports as Honorary Director of the National Equestrian Centre since its inception, and as one of the most experienced Masters of Foxhounds.

Therefore, we have included topical surveys of the challenge facing the Equestrian Centre, the gold medal chances of Britain's three-day event team, and the problems and joys of modern fox hunting.

As one who rides for fun, but thoroughly enjoys competitive horse sports as a spectator, I have had much pleasure in working with Dorian on this book. Our aim is to share with you some of the fun which is given in such abundance by our great friend – the horse.

Michael Clayton

"I CAN'T REMEMBER A BETTER YEAR"

Woe, woe, woe . . . it is surprising how much of it is being preached in some parts of the world of show jumping.

The 1972 Olympic Games draws closer, and already the defeatists are predicting the worst for Britain. We shan't have the horses; our preparation and selection methods are wrong; we shall never beat the Germans on their home ground . . . These are the sort of things you hear from some people much involved in British show jumping.

Of course there is no room for complacency. Yet we have less excuse for defeatism than any other country in the world.

At the start of the '71 season Britain was at a peak of achievement in show jumping.

Colonel Sir Mike Ansell, chairman of the British Show Jumping Association, reported: "I believe the stimulus of our sport, or for that matter any sport, is provided by success of British riders.

"Nineteen seventy has been perhaps one of our greatest, if not the greatest. Certainly, I cannot remember a better.

"In the world championships, out of the six medals we have won four – a gold, a silver and two bronze – and above all we have regained the President's Cup for the third time in six years.

"Perhaps the outstanding part of this success has been that the four Nations Cups, and the 42 individual international competitions have been won by no less than 47 different British horses and 20 riders.

"David Broome, the World champion, already European champion, Harvey Smith, the winner of two classics in Britain and outstanding in the President's Cup, Marion Mould and Anneli Drummond-Hay–all are supreme.

"Yet perhaps, looking to the future, it has been a more superb season because among those who have come right to the fore are five riders under 23-years-old. There is no nation in the world with such a reserve and let no-one forget that we won the European Junior Championships against 18 nations. In fact, we have almost swept the board."

Ah yes, say the critics. But can we keep it up? Horses don't last forever. Some of the leading horses which have given us so much success certainly will be past their best performances before the Olympic Games in Munich.

We can derive much comfort from Sir Mike Ansell's point that 47 horses represented Britain in international contests during a highly successful season. Yet this does not bring unrelieved joy to our selectors, since their task is not simply a matter of matching the very best horses available to the most successful and experienced riders.

Human nature has to be considered, as well as equine performance. How often in the past have there been squabbles when owners have been approached to allow horses to take part in an Olympic team as mounts for leading riders.

The problem can occur when the owner is himself not a rider, but it is even more likely when the horse has an owner-rider who has not been selected for the Olympics through being under age, or lacking in experience of top international events.

Despite the pressure of "patriotic duty" it is indeed a considerable sacrifice to give a horse as a possible Olympic mount. Having been short-listed, the horse has to be allowed a much easier season at home during the summer before the Olympic Games, and this may entail a considerable loss in prize money. The long distance to be travelled to some Olympic Games, is another factor which deters some owners, and who can blame them, since a horse can easily be upset by such a journey, having its subsequent form ruined for the following season. The risk of injuries with permanent ill-effects is far from negligible over a massive Olympic course.

One other problem for the owner asked to contribute a horse to the Olympic effort, is that after carefully nursing the animal through a season by cutting down its competitions, the horse may at a later stage be rejected in favour of another, and the sacrifice in possible prize money will have been in vain.

Most of these problems should be lessened to some extent in '72 since the travelling risks are much reduced in having to take horses to Munich, instead of Mexico or Tokyo. Acclimatisation will be no problem, and leading horses and riders are well used to travelling all over the continent.

Sir Michael Ansell congratulates Capt. R. d'Inzeo (Italy), after winning the Moss Bros' Championship

Marion Coakes (now Mrs. Mould) and Stroller

The West Germans can probably be relied upon, more than any other country in the world, to organise their equestrian events properly.

They are building an Olympic village at Riem, near Munich airport, with stabling for 400 horses. It will have a wonderful training area, comprising seven jumping paddocks, six dressage arenas and two covered maneges.

The show jumping team event will be held in the main Olympic stadium, and the individual show jumping will be in a special equestrian stadium being built in the Olympic grounds. It will accommodate more than 30,000 spectators. The Olympic dressage will take place in the Nymphenburger Schlosspark, and the three-day event cross country course is being built between the areas of Riem and Poing.

The dressage will have an appropriately elegant, historic setting, since it is in the grounds of the Nymphenburg Palace, built in 1663. Remounts for the rulers of Bavaria were broken-in there in the 18th century.

All Olympic horses will certainly have every comfort when not competing. The Germans have designed a new type of stable in which grooms can keep a constant watch on their horses, from above the boxes in

12

Harvey Smith and Evan Jones in the Wills Castella Stakes

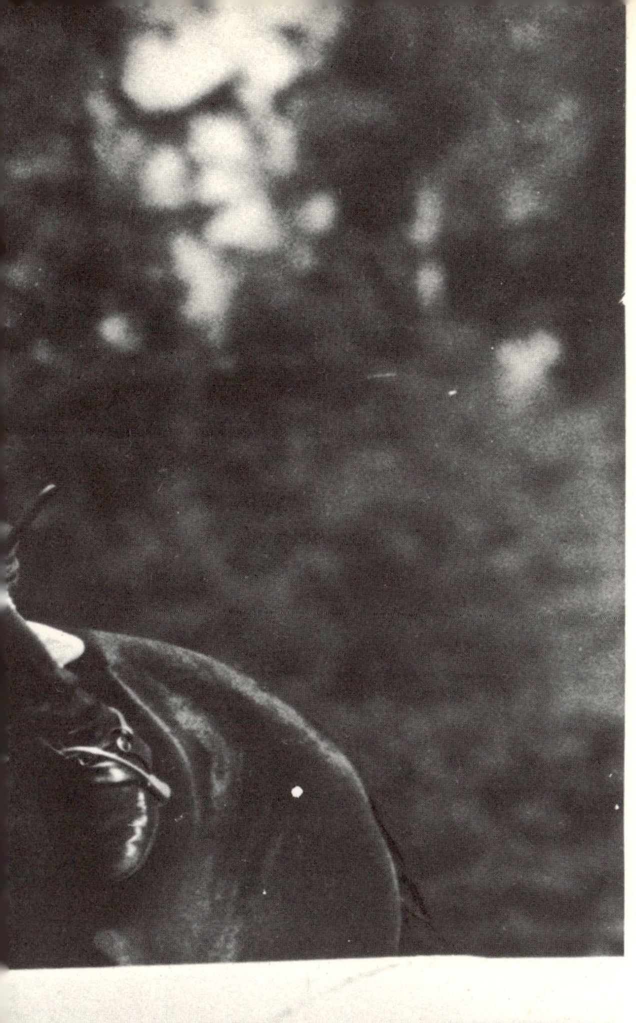

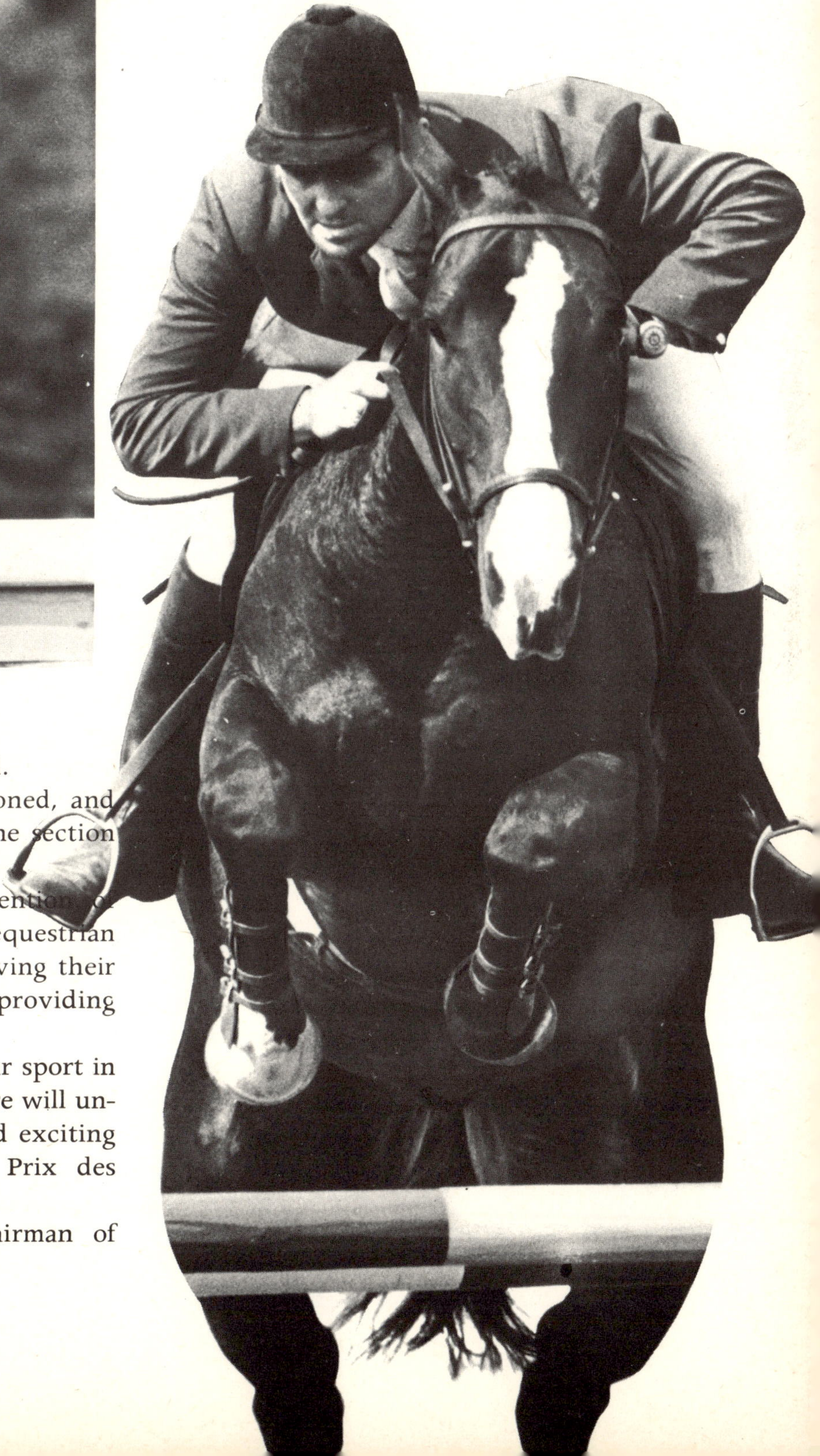

which they will be accommodated.

The stables will be air conditioned, and include a sick-bay with quarantine section and a veterinary surgery box.

The Germans have every intention of snatching the major share of the equestrian medals, but they are certainly giving their rivals the best possible chance by providing superb facilities.

Show Jumping is such a popular sport in West Germany that the atmosphere will undoubtedly be extremely tense and exciting during the individual and the Prix des Nations classes.

Colonel Harry Llewellyn, chairman of

Britain's International Selection Committee, says, "I have every confidence we will have a tremendous chance of winning the gold medal in Munich, although we must not delude ourselves that the German team on its home ground will not be a tough nut to crack".

David Broome, 1970 winner of the World Championship title, rates the German chances of gold medals very highly, and thinks the United States will be the other contender for the top honours. He also emphasises the enormous part luck plays in show jumping, and there is plenty of evidence of this in previous Olympic Games.

In Mexico, Britain's excellent chances of winning the team class were blitzed by the sheer misfortune of Marion Mould's Stroller suffering a decayed tooth and sinus trouble which made him jump well below form. Those who claimed dramatically that the little pony had "jumped his heart out" have

Anneli Drummond-Hay and Xanthos during the Wills Embassy Stakes

had their answer many times since then. Stroller's 1970 season was one of his best ever, and included his fantastic victory in the Hamburg Jumping Derby when he beat some of the world's best horses by achieving the only clear round over the notoriously difficult course.

One thing is certain about the '72 Olympics: Stroller will not be competing again, and nor will Marion, since she has repeatedly affirmed that Mexico was her first and last Olympic Games. Since she achieved a silver medal in the individual class, she can well afford to abandon further Olympic ambitions, and anyway at the time of writing she has no Olympic class horse as a replacement for the veteran Stroller.

Barring accidents or some other misfortune, it is hard to imagine the selectors being able to relinquish Marion's two team mates: David Broome and Harvey Smith. After his world championship win, where he demonstrated his superb talent on other people's horses as well as his own mount, David clinched the verdict of many experts after his previous season's European championship win. The verdict is simply that he is the best show jumping rider in the world.

Harvey has the facility to bring on an extraordinary number of promising new horses. No-one could ever accuse him of being a "one horse" star, even though he has had such remarkable individual animals in his string of mounts. His problem is in ensuring that one of them is rested and at peak form at the time of the Olympics. He puts his own stamp of extreme obedience and control on his horses, but if anything his style has become somewhat more fluid than it was some years ago, and his virtuosity over puissance or speed courses is legendary.

Apart from their sheer skill, it would be

Caroline Bradley and Franco at the treble

difficult to discard Broome or Smith because of their enormous experience of the big occasion. Just as a football team can be mesmerised and over-awed by the Wembley roar on Cup final day, so can a show jumping rider be overcome by the sense of occasion when for the first time he or she rides into an Olympic arena all alone, knowing the fate of a whole team depends on a good round and above all, avoidance of elimination.

The ability to ride coolly and accurately in these conditions is vital in an Olympic Games. For these reasons, the brilliant intuitive Welsh rider, and the tough, persistent Yorkshireman, must be almost certain of selection for the '72 Olympics – unless some malignant fate intervenes.

Who would accompany them? Here, the permutations become much more difficult.

By virtue of sheer international experience, and expertise, Anneli Drummond-Hay springs to mind, but at the end of the 1970 season her possible Olympic class horse, Sporting Ford, had not been particularly convincing as a candidate for Munich. There was still plenty of time for further evidence of ability from this horse, or possibly for Anneli to produce a better alternative.

The selectors' task is eased to some extent, in that for the first time four riders may take part on behalf of each country, the best three scores to count. Until now, only three riders competed, the fourth member of the team attending the Games as a reserve for late inclusion in the team in the event of unfitness.

This new decision was made at the end of 1970 by the international ruling body, the Federation Equestre Internationale, meeting in Brussels with Prince Philip in the chair as its president.

The F.E.I. also ruled that only the eight best placed teams in the first round of the team event may compete in the second round. The classification would be obtained by adding together the scores of the best three competitors of these teams in each round.

Thus the prospect of four competing riders opens up much better prospects for the impressive group of younger riders who came to the fore so much during Britain's wonderful 1970 season. They include Anne Moore, Michael Saywell, Graham Fletcher, Raymond Howe, and Stephen Hadley. The somewhat better known names of Caroline Bradley and Anne Backhouse (nee Townsend) must also figure on a selectors' list.

With four riders in the team instead of three, the selectors can surely take a chance on at least one brilliant young rider who may, or may not, rise to the big occasion. Much will depend on whether that young rider has a real Olympic type mount.

The horse which can win consistently at

Anne Backhouse and Cardinal jumping at Hickstead

County shows may prove utterly useless over an Olympic course. For the contrast between the conventional course of temporary fences, and the specially built international course has widened still further in recent years.

Olympic fences are massive, and in terms of sheer courage, apart from innate ability, an Olympic class horse has to be exceptional. The combination of three jumps which defeated Stroller in Mexico was a 5 feet 3 inches wall, followed by parallel poles at 4 feet 9 inches high with a 5 feet 4 inches spread, then more parallel poles of 5 feet by 6 feet.

Any hesitation or loss of impulsion between these fences meant immediate disaster at the next obstacle. Stroller, burdened by his illness, could not quite make it after jumping the wall, falling down in attempting to jump the first parallel. Yet he *did* jump the whole combination at a second attempt.

The Germans have long concentrated on producing big horses capable of tackling the most massive of courses, and entirely leaving aside the case of Stroller, who is a unique phenomenon at only 14·2 hands. Britain will need large horses of great scope to tackle the Munich courses.

Trying to predict Olympic horses accurately at this stage is a hopeless task, but it is worth bearing in mind that David Broome's world championship mount, Beethoven, will be 14-years-old in '72, which is by no means old for a show jumper. Harvey Smith's Mattie Brown has grown even better since Mexico, and put up some wonderful performances in 1970, finishing second in the list of the top ten horses of the season. Archie and Gold Point are other Harvey Smith mounts which have real potential, and he has other prospects.

Graham Fletcher's six-year-old Buttevant Boy, and his eight-year-old Talk of the North have been most impressive. Mr T. Banks' Hideaway, the partner of Michael Saywell, is hardly a quality horse, but he seems to have enormous scope and consistency over big fences.

The contrast between international jumping and much of the home circuit is shown by the apparently paradoxical situation in which Alan Oliver, winner of the B.S.J.A.

Alan Oliver and Pitz Palu in the European Championships at Hickstead

National Championship, with Sweep, did not represent Britain in a Nations Cup event in 1970.

Yet with Pitz Palu, Alan headed the season's list of prize winning horses. He is indeed the specialist in speed classes, and tours the circuit of county shows, and other major shows, relentlessly pursuing victory with his excellent string of horses, belonging to Mr and Mrs Cawthraw. Yet, significantly, Alan does not nowadays choose to jump at Hickstead, the only permanent course in Britain equal to the big courses on the continent.

With his long experience and skill, Alan could probably achieve considerable success again as a major international star. In 1969 he won two contests in Rome and was a member of the team which won the Nations Cup in Barcelona. Yet by concentrating most of his effort on the domestic scene, Alan notches up a tremendous string of successes each season.

Those who appear in the top ten list do win thousands of pounds worth of prizes each season, but they are a very small minority, since there are some 7,000 horses and ponies registered as jumpers in Britain. Few can even cover their costs, let alone make a profit. As Col. Sir Mike Ansell says: "Show jumping is an expensive sport; the keep of a horse is very different from that of a bicycle or a set of golf clubs.

"Much nonsense is talked about prize money, and although the prize money is now large, it in no way covers costs. There aren't many horses winning over £2,000, and to come out square you have got to win about £1,500. That won't cover the cost of bringing on a young horse for the future."

All this is relevant to the Olympic competition, since even with sponsorship of leading events, and the private patronage of some generous owners, British Olympic teams are at something of a disadvantage compared to some foreign countries where the private patronage is wealthier, or where the government makes a substantial contribution to costs.

In the United States the equestrian team enjoys permanent training facilities at Gladstone, New Jersey. Coached by Bertalan de Nemethy, the U.S. show jumpers have achieved remarkable style and quality in their performances.

In West Germany it is not so much wealthy patronage as sheer popular enthusiasm which has helped to achieve her superb post war record. A portion of admission charges at all jumping competitions is contributed to the German Olympic fund which has become extremely rich and helps buy suitable horses.

Some indication of the sort of price which can be paid on the international market for top-grade show jumpers was shown towards the end of the 1970 season when the champagne firm, Moet and Chandon, gave a reported £30,000 for the 10-years-old gelding Morning Light, sold to them by Iris Kellett of Dublin.

The horse was bought for the great French rider Pierre Jonqueres d'Oriola, the only man to win two individual Olympic gold medals for show jumping. Earlier in 1970 he had been without a suitable mount for the world championship at La Baule. The champagne firm have certainly done their best to rectify matters for the '72 Olympics.

Money cannot solve all problems in show jumping by any means, but it definitely helps. The French rider Janou Lefebvre's mount Rocket, with which she won the Women's world championship, was bought for her for £20,000.

In Britain far more of our top riders are likely to have bought a young horse for less than £1,000 and "made" it themselves. The temptation to sell the horse later at an enormous profit to an overseas buyer, must be very great sometimes. It is to the credit of British riders and owners that it is frequently resisted, although such sales do augment the incomes of some leading show jumpers considerably.

Yet if there was a ruthless policy of selling horses whenever possible, British show jumping would soon be very much the poorer. One of the best examples of this was Marion Mould's decision to turn down a £30,000 American offer for Stroller the year *before* the Mexico Olympics when they won a silver medal for Britain.

Fortunately, after weighing up the pros and cons very carefully, no leading British rider in 1970 took advantage of the F.E.I.'s new regulations which allowed professionals to compete in virtually all amateur competitions – except the Olympic Games.

Some riders pointed out that the financial

Pierre Jonqueres d'Oriola and Nagir, during the Individual Grand Prix—at the Olympic Games,

advantages of turning professional were extremely doubtful anyway, since a professional is immediately subject to income tax requirements which do not apply to an amateur who is only supposed to sell three competition horses in one year.

Yet despite such practical reasons as these, the leading riders also made it plain they would sorely miss the opportunity of riding for Britain in an Olympic Games. It's still a coveted honour – and Britain's best riders will be doing their darndest to prove the defeatists so wrong at Munich in '72.

Even if you and I cannot be there, we shall no doubt see and hear it all – with the aid of Dorian Williams and BBC television.

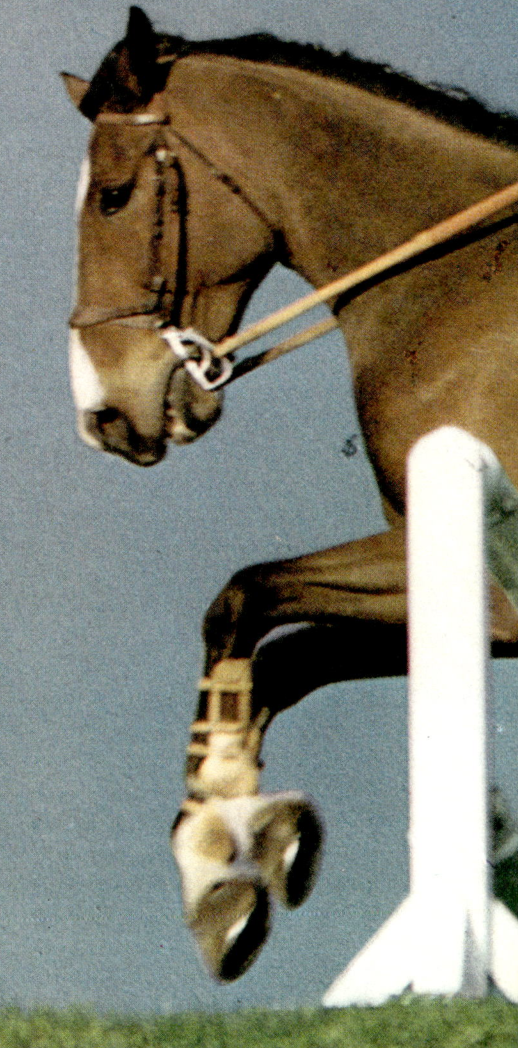

Harvey Smith and Ten To Twelve, in the Wills Parcours De Chasse, at Hickstead

ANOTHER TEN YEARS

The 1971 season marks the start of a second decade for the All-England Jumping Course at Hickstead in Sussex.

Everyone in the world of show jumping knows Hickstead, and nowadays the vast majority recognise the tremendous contribution this permanent course has made in its first decade to the standard of British show jumping.

Soon many millions of TV viewers will be aware of the special atmosphere of this wonderful course which was the brainchild of Douglas Bunn, the barrister and business-man who made a great impact on the sport which he first enjoyed as a competitor.

He has signed a new contract with the BBC which will ensure national showing of Hickstead's famous events of which the most spectacular is the British Jumping Derby. Hitherto Hickstead was televised regularly by the local commercial company, Southern Independent Television, and Douglas Bunn pays tribute to their coverage in helping to put Hickstead on the map.

When he opened his course in May, 1960, few at first appreciated the value of the enormous arena with its unusual obstacles.

Until then British show jumping had been dominated by the annual county shows where the show jumping courses were temporary fences erected each year, and they usually showed little variety or imagination in their construction. Yet on the continent British riders found they had to contend with banks, walls and ditches instead of the conventional gates and poles they jumped at home.

Douglas, known as Douggie throughout the show jumping world, recalls riding for Britain in the 'fifties when they visited Germany: "We spent all our time getting our horses used to the course instead of trying to win. The only person who did not have this problem in those days was Pat Smythe who continually went abroad to all those continental jumping grounds."

Douglas Bunn – the man who helped put Hickstead on the map

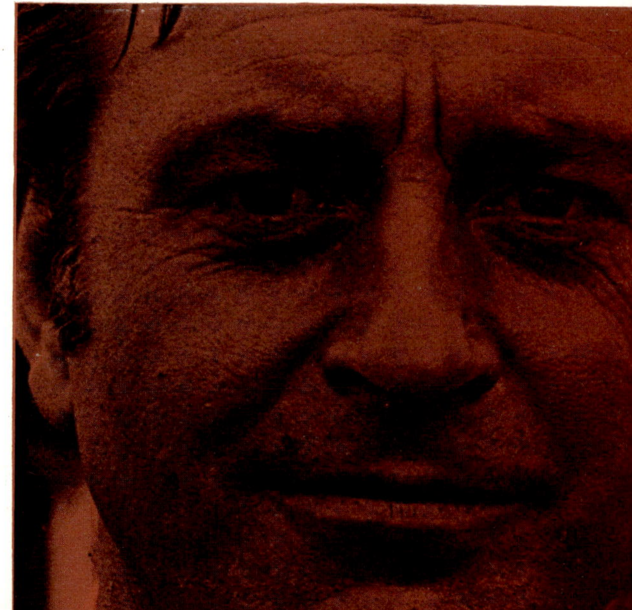

Aileen Ross and Beaudlare, on the bank at Hickstead

To Bunn the problem seemed clear: we could never take on the Germans with a chance of winning unless we were as well equipped as they were with permanent courses.

So he built his course in the winter of 1959, in the grounds of his house, Hickstead Place, by the main Brighton-London road. The course included an open water jump, water ditch, a "table", Devil's Dyke, and a bank – not the famous Derby bank which came later.

Douglas Bunn says: "I tried to create a big show, but still retain the small show atmosphere. I felt the days of the big stadium were over. More people wanted to take their cars with them everywhere and we made ample provision for people to watch this first class show jumping from their own ring-side car park positions."

Some laughed, some even sneered when Douglas dared to call his new venture the All-England Jumping Course right from the start. The critics did not think it would last long, and certainly the signs of support were far from encouraging. When entries closed for the opening show at Hickstead the number of entries numbered – just one!

Some hasty 'phoning produced about 30 entrants turning up for the first day of a

David Broome and Top of The Morning at Hickstead

three-day show. There were only six cars in the spectators' car park area. The first six horses jumping the Hickstead course were eliminated after refusing at the variety of obstacles. Then from the West Country came Tom Brake, riding into the ring on Bill Reece's Cubhunter. Tom "hunted" round the ring as if he was taking a young horse out following hounds for the first time. He got round, and "broke the ice".

1

There was a great roar of applause as Tom left the ring. "There you are, that's the way to ride round this", said Tom. And everyone present decided they had better have a go. Hickstead lost a lot of money on its first show, but Douggie Bunn felt encouraged enough to go on. His foresight and enterprise have since been rewarded with one of the most remarkable success stories in post-war British sport.

Entries increased with every meeting. Almost all top riders automatically included the Hickstead meetings in their programme. W. D. & H. O. Wills undertook sponsorship of Hickstead towards the end of the first season and have done so ever since. Soon the course attained considerable international status, and some of the best overseas show jumpers have appeared there frequently.

The chance to ride the Hickstead course is now accepted as an important factor in the upswing in Britain's fortunes on the continent after 1961. Leading international events have also been allotted to Hickstead, including the Ladies World Championship in 1965, won by Marion Mould and Stroller, and the European championship in '69, captured by David Broome and Mr Softce.

The famous British Jumping Derby started in 1961, and there have only been ten clear rounds over the mile long course with 16 formidable jumps, the best known obstacle being the famous Derby bank. Douglas Bunn paid a New Year's Eve visit to the famous Hamburg Jumping Derby Course, first built in 1918, and measured their enormous bank. Then he came back and constructed his own Derby bank slightly higher at 11 feet, with its formidably steep slope at one end where the horses have to descend and then tackle a fence very quickly.

If there is a "King" of Hickstead it must be little Stroller, Marion Mould's famous pony.

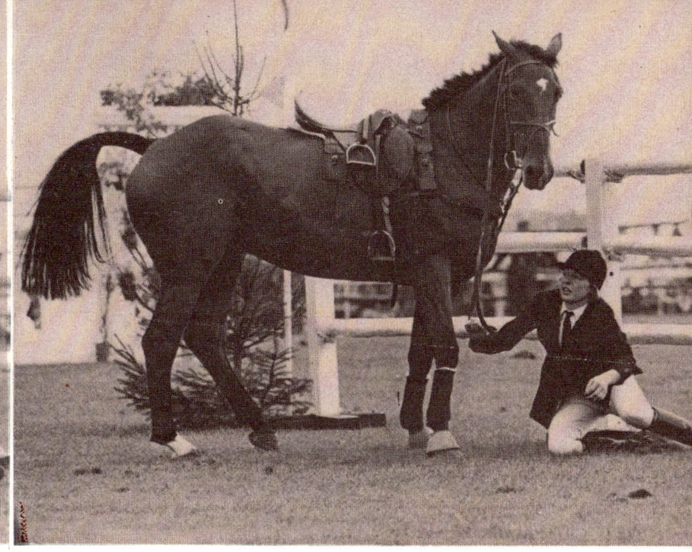

Caroline Bradley and Errigal in trouble at the Jumping Derby

Together they won the Jumping Derby in 1967 and they have notched up three of the ten clear rounds on the course.

Stroller, despite his comparatively diminutive size, revels in the wide open spaces of Hickstead, striding on between fences in masterly fashion and soaring confidently over every fence. He is a great favourite with Hickstead crowds, and his amazing consistency over the big courses is shown by his extraordinary record in winning with Marion the Wills Hickstead Gold Medal, awarded for most points achieved there during a season, for five consecutive years.

Douglas Bunn says small active horses with courage and great scope are especially well suited to Derby courses. The 1969 winner, Anneli Drummond-Hay's Xanthos, was another example of this type of jumper. Victory last season went to Harvey Smith for the first time in the Jumping Derby; his mount, Mattie Brown.

Hickstead has always placed a strong accent on youth, and while the international

More trouble in the Derby . . . for John Kidd and Grey Owl

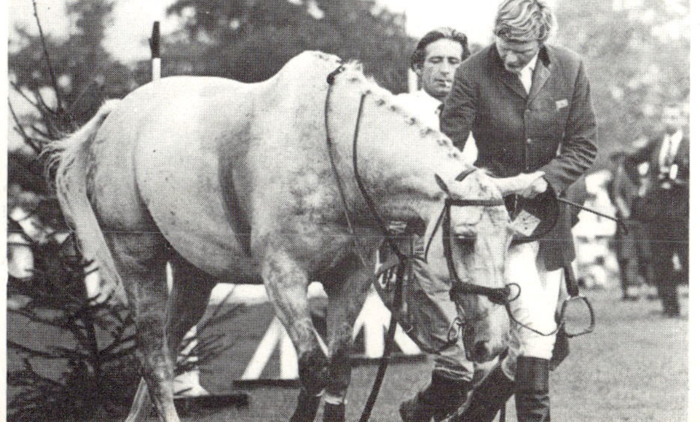

◀ Anne Backhouse and Brigadier having a not-so-happy landing

1

Anneli Drummond-Hay and Big George in the Wills Hickstead Tankard

2

stars thrill the crowds in the big arena, equally important show jumping, in terms of future performances, is going on in the three rings nearby where there are excellent, well built courses for a many novice and intermediate events.

For other riding enthusiasts there is the annual attraction of the British Dressage Derby, and the British Driving Derby provides the elegance of the hackney each year.

Douglas Bunn is always thinking ahead and Hickstead is due for some exciting developments in its second decade. During the 1970–71 winter a block of superbly equipped private viewing boxes were being erected next to the Hickstead club house at the ring side, but apart from the small club stand the remainder of the ring-side area is still open for cars and picknicking spectators, giving the show a delightfully informal atmosphere despite its international standards inside the ring.

Classes for show hunters, with a specially built series of jumps for them, were to be an innovation in 1971. But the major coup was

the decision to transfer the Royal International Horse Show's Prince of Wales (Nations) Cup event from Wembley to Hickstead. It was taking place on the Sunday preceding the International's Tuesday opening at the Empire Pool building, Wembley, where the jumping now takes place indoors.

Sir Michael Ansell, director of the Royal International, said in announcing the move he was sure Mr Bunn would give the Nations' Cup "every dignity it deserves".

"I can promise you", he said, "that neither I nor Douglas Bunn has climbed down in any way. But it is ridiculous for two great shows to be at loggerheads and the solution that has been found is common sense for show jumping."

It was a good sign for the future of British show jumping when Sir Michael said he and Douglas Bunn were going to "pull together" to make the new arrangement a success. For the leading international riders, British and visitors from overseas, it will mean a busy nine days – four days jumping out of

3

4

doors at Hickstead, with the Prince of Wales Cup as the major event between teams representing each country; then five days indoors at the Empire Pool, Wembley, for the Royal International.

There was some criticism of the Royal International's venue, indoors in 1970 for the first time for many years, after show jumping was banned from the Wembley stadium turf in the interests of football.

Some observers feel the move of the Prince of Wales Cup to Hickstead is a big step towards holding the complete Royal International show there, but it would be extremely premature to make such a prediction. Despite the criticisms, the 1970 Royal International was overall a great success, with enthusiastic audiences at all evening sessions ensuring satisfaction at the box office. The show had a different atmosphere from the end of the season Horse of the Year Show, even though both are now held at the same place.

Most B.S.J.A. top officials feel strongly that every effort should be made to retain the leading show of the year in the capital. The Empire Pool building is not ideal, especially while some of the showing classes have to be held outside, but the show executive seems prepared to continue there until a better alternative becomes available – in London.

From a practical point of view, those who maintained the experience of jumping indoors in the middle of the season would harm the prospects of our team when they next jumped out of doors, were proved wrong. Britain won the Prince of Wales Cup indoors at Wembley, and then went off to Dublin the following week to win the Aga Khan Trophy in the Nations Cup contest, in the open at Ballsbridge.

Whatever the future of the Royal International, Hickstead's important role in British show jumping is assured. It has its own special atmosphere, and in its second decade will continue to help British riders gain the vital experience over a big, permanent course, so necessary if we are to retain our position among the international leaders.

Above; at Badminton, the Earl of St. Andrew finds it thirsty work watching the horse trials. Below, left; H.R.H. The Queen Mother presents Richard Meade with the Whitbread Saddle, he won on "The Poacher". Below, right; Lord Snowdon attentively watches the Badminton Trials.

CHALLENGE IN THE HUNTING FIELD

The challenge of foxhunting is as alive today as ever. Many outside the world of horse and hound, do not realise there is more, *rather than less hunting compared with the 18th and 19th centuries.*

A list of packs of foxhounds published about 170 years ago shows only 95 Hunts; there are now almost 200. The number of Hunts increased rapidly since the 1930's because in the immediate post war years it was difficult to transport horses and hounds to meets over a wide area. This led to some hunts splitting up into smaller units.

Every war has been followed by an extraordinary upsurge in hunting's popularity, as thousands of ex-servicemen and women turned thankfully to the pleasures of riding to hounds in our still glorious countryside.

The boom in all forms of horse riding over the last 20 years has brought a host of newcomers to the hunting field, relishing its challenge to the horseman, and in many cases also appreciating the skills and satisfactions of hunting itself. The latter is almost impossible to communicate to anyone who has not hunted.

Yet now the trend has turned: hunts are beginning to face closures or amalgamations. During the 1970's the trend is likely to accelerate still more.

"Ah, I suppose it's the anti-hunting movement which is the big problem", sagely remark one's non-hunting friends.

Although the possibility of parliamentary action by those opposed to field sports is something which always has to be faced, it is in practical terms the *least* of the problems facing hunting today.

Loss of countryside through new towns, roads and airports, is the biggest enemy to hunting. It is, of course, a much wider issue. Ruining our countryside by thoughtless expansion is a crime against society as a whole.

The sharply increasing costs of hunting is another big problem in maintaining the sport, but this is not insuperable, and is certainly eased by sensible hunt amalgamations where the use of hunt stables and kennels are centralised.

Foxhunting's problem, especially in surviving rural areas near the big areas of population, is that more people want to hunt than can reasonably be accommodated. A Hunt has to place some limit on the number of its mounted followers in the interests of its hosts – the farmers and landowners on whose land the pack runs.

Most hunting takes place on privately owned land; without the co-operation of tenants and owners, hunting would virtually cease overnight in most areas of Britain.

Those who assert that hunting is "not so popular" in the modern countryside should ponder on this fact, which is all the more significant in view of the increasing number of farmers who are owner-occupiers.

A classic example of the way hunting's fortunes are inextricably combined with the fate of the British countryside, was the proposal to build the third London airport at Cublington in Buckinghamshire, virtually destroying the fabric of country life throughout the surrounding area.

The Whaddon Chase, of which Dorian Williams is Joint Master, would have lost its fine, grass vale, with timber and fly fences, which have delighted generations of sportsmen and women. A Hunt such as the Whaddon Chase provides a focal point for a host of social activities in the countryside: the local point-to-point, farmer's suppers, hunter trials, supporters' club functions, and Pony Club activities.

The fight for rural Britain is inevitably hunting's own battle for survival; the two go hand in hand. A distinguished writer on point-to-point racing, remarked in an otherwise excellent book published recently he was getting "just a little tired of the ceaseless propaganda that is being poured by the British Field Sports Society with their incessant warnings that the end of foxhunting would mean the end of point-to-point racing".

He felt point-to-point racing would still survive "in one form or another", and remarked "after all, there are always the draghunts".

There is a massive argument against this short-sighted viewpoint. One aspect is that only seven packs of drag-hounds are listed nowadays, compared with 14 before the war; so drag-hunting is hardly on the increase, and two of the existing drag-hunts are attached to universities, two are military, and one is in Jersey, leaving only two ordinary subscription packs.

Drag-hunting – following an artificial line, dragged across country beforehand – can be great fun, but bears very little similarity to foxhunting. At its best, drag-hunting is like a steeple-chase across country, and can only be enjoyed by small fields, extremely

well mounted. Foxhunting has a much more universal appeal; to the young and old; to those who like to "go", and those who are happy to jog about enjoying watching hounds; and it provides a much longer day out in the country.

Point-to-point racing needs a broad base of support throughout a country area which only foxhunting can provide, and if it is used properly the genuine hunting field with its variety of pace, and its opportunity of hunting throughout the week, is still the best place to "bring on" a young horse for point-to-point racing, or for horse trials and show jumping.

Many young, flighty, thoroughbreds – ill disciplined and useless for any controlled activity – have settled down during a careful season in the hunting field, and have then gone on to success in three day events or international show jumping contests.

The hunting field still provides wonderful cross country riding experience and acts as a reservoir for equine talent. Many a working hunter has shown exceptional ability in the hunting field, and has gone on to fame on the race course or in other competitive horse sports. Many a Grand National winner is basically a good hunter.

Because the hunting field requires so many thousands of horses each year, many more are bred than those which graduate to show jumping or eventing. This gives Britain a tremendous advantage over her international rivals. It is the reason why foreigners go to Ireland or England in search of their horses; sometimes we are beaten by Irish or English bred horses wearing a foreign flag on their saddle flaps.

Britain's supremacy in show jumping and three day eventing was heavily emphasised in 1970, but if foreign competitors were restricted to using only horses bred in their own countries, British dominance would be even more complete. Not that I am advocating such restrictions on foreigners, since the ability to sell horses abroad at high prices is a valuable incentive to breeders in this country who need every possible encouragement.

An opening meet of the Old Berkeley—now part of the Vale of Aylesbury Hunt

In reverse, the hunting field acts as a haven for the horse who has not quite made it as a show jumper, eventer or race horse. Often, freed of the cramping restrictions of the competitive world, such a horse will make a superb hunter, providing years of enjoyment for his lucky rider, and obviously the horse is happy too.

Most horsemen or women experience "the horse of a lifetime"; the animal with which one is particularly in tune, and has provided one's most memorable hours in the saddle.

Frequently, a hunting man's "horse of a lifetime" is a mount which has had a somewhat chequered career outside the hunting field, and has then found his true metier following hounds. Sadly, your reporter has just retired such a horse, after nearly ten seasons together in the hunting field.

He is a rather cobby, blue roan, with a wonderful front, but not quite enough substance behind the saddle. He has one "big knee" from some youthful accident, and for years his feet had a tendency to split. Yet he was the most wonderful hunter: bold, yet clever in tackling any kind of jump, and able to hunt until darkness in any going. Gates, iron railings, fly fences and massive drop fences were all challenges he would meet with ears pricked, a superbly timed take-off and enormous scope for a half-bred horse. He did not have the speed of a Shires blood hunter, but his jumping ability and stamina enabled him to keep his place at the front of the field in many different provincial countries.

Now, at 18, an old liver complaint has worsened, sapping his stamina at last, so that he is not up to a full day's hunting carrying my weight. But he will never be a quiet ride; he still takes a massive hold until he is in front of the field, and will take the biggest fences as bravely as ever.

Fortunately, he thrives on an outdoor life, thanks to a rugged upbringing on rough grazing in Ireland. He now lives in a paddock next to the hunting stables, where he is treasured as a real "character", and carefully observes all that is happening in stables. He looks more than a trifle wistful when I appear in scarlet coat and silk hat and ride off on his younger successors, but perhaps I am falling into the trap of sentimentality. As long as he shows signs of thriving and enjoying life, he will continue as a respected pensioner. He certainly owes me nothing; the debt is mine.

Dorian Williams' favourite old hunter, Gay Galliard – a wild eyed chestnut which pulled like a train – settled down in the hunting field to become as kind, generous and responsive a horse as Dorian could ever remember. Previously, Gay Galliard had won in the show ring, but had become so hot he could not be relied on in the hands of a judge. He had started jumping, but after a short spell had gone sour and refused even to enter the ring. Out hunting he took such a hold that he was scarcely safe, and having once raced he had become hotter and wilder than ever. The horse went well for Dorian because pullers seldom give trouble when ridden without horses in front of them, and Dorian's role as Master meant keeping in front of the rest of the mounted field as much as possible.

For the horseman, the challenge of the hunting field is still one of the paramount attractions of riding in Britain. It is the most common bond between people who, at other times of the year, practice widely different branches of horsemanship.

Yet in the years ahead we shall have to

adjust to some inevitable changes and retractions in the pattern of hunting. Dorian Williams feels it is vital to the survival and success of foxhunting in the future that it should be so managed that Hunts do not get into trouble near Britain's still growing towns and cities.

Masters have to be realistic, remembering that hunting is a country sport and will always be acceptable in the countryside, but it is not surprising that hunting can run into difficulties in urban areas, where people are not necessarily opposed to it, but where they are ignorant of country sports.

"If we try to carry on hunting in a country which is no longer 'huntable' we must not be surprised if we sometimes get a bad Press", says Dorian.

There is still plenty of suitable hunting country in many areas of Britain, but if hunting is to be managed realistically in future there must inevitably be certain reorganisation to avoid increasing urban development.

So the future seems to offer slightly less hunting available, but every effort is being made to ensure the highest possible standard. The quality of the modern foxhound is better than ever, and this is a crucial factor in the survival of the sport. Yet there is no need to think in terms of mere survival. Even with some retraction, foxhunting still shows every sign of flourishing for generations to come.

Henry Fielding's verse written in 1734 will still have a contemporary ring:

"The dusky night rides down the sky,
  And ushers in the morn;
  The Hounds all join the glorious cry,
  The Huntsman winds his horn
  And a-Hunting we will go!"

"He's asked for political asylum."

Courtesy of "Punch"

THE WAY AHEAD

Hard times ahead; the warning light is being flashed for some established summer shows which have long played a part in the show jumping season.

Is it going to mean less opportunities for young up and coming show jumpers in the 1970's? The possibility arises because the total membership of the British Show Jumping Association continues to rise each year, amounting to more than 9,700 at the end of 1970. There was an increase of 479 during 1970, of which half were juniors.

More show jumpers; less shows – how is the B.S.J.A. to cope?

Col. Sir Mike Ansell pointed out: "I believe we should be prepared for the number of shows falling, due to rising costs, and in particular the possible drop of trade exhibits, which provide a very valuable income to Agricultural Shows.

"I believe we should expect a number of the smaller one-day shows to find it difficult to continue, and possibly to have to amalgamate."

The B.S.J.A. has seen the warning light of rising costs. Show jumping, being an expensive sport, is especially vulnerable to the rising tide of inflation.

Labour in stables, forage, shoeing, vet's bills, transport to shows . . . it is a formidable list of expenses for anyone keeping horses nowadays. Will it be worth keeping novice horses if there are fewer shows worth attending in future?

Most of the 7,000 registered show jumping horses in Britain are novices, and need plenty of opportunities for experience in the ring.

The B.S.J.A. thinks the answer may be the formation of Equestrian Sports Clubs on the lines of one being formed at Windsor. Members would compete monthly on Smith's Lawn, and it was hoped there would be facilities for combined training, dressage and driving as well as show jumping.

Sir Mike says: "The object will be to provide an opportunity for bringing on young horses, and for inexperienced riders to have fun. Big prize money is not visualised; probably, it will mean only competing for sweepstakes.

"I hope and believe the B.S.J.A. will do all in its power to encourage these sports clubs, for it is from the four thousand young Grade C horses we will find our future international winners."

Some agricultural societies with permanent show grounds are forming equestrian sports clubs, including the Great Yorkshire and the Bath and West.

If the equestrian clubs flourish – and there will have to be scores or even hundreds of them before they can be said to have succeeded widely – they will mean less emphasis in future on the "pot hunting" element in show jumping.

Ever since motor transport made it easier for a rider to take his horses far afield show jumping has meant that top riders tour a regular circuit of leading shows, dominating all the top placings in the main events.

This has helped to raise standards by giving local people opportunities to see the best riders in action, and to compete against them. To some extent the well known show jumpers are crowd-pullers, and benefit the show organisers by ensuring peak interest in the jumping events. This appeal has lessened somewhat in recent years, and some shows have turned to other attractions ranging from trick motor cycling to parachute jumping to lure the public to the ringside.

In the equestrian clubs the show jumpers will not be part of a programme of public entertainment. Anyone watching will be a club supporter, or a show jumping enthusiast. Since novices do not win enough money to "earn their keep" anyway, their owners will hardly be worse off by competing for sweepstake prizes.

The most welcome part of the B.S.J.A.'s plan is that riders should attend the equestrian club meetings for fun as well as experience. In the tough road to the top it is so easy to forget the fun. The inexperienced rider will be less tempted to emulate the leading show jumpers in chasing the prize money and rosettes from one show to the next if he or she can get regular competition experience in the club. Of course, they will still attend other shows, but they can afford to be more selective.

The prospect of these clubs holding other horse activities such as eventing may also help young riders avoid specialising too early. Many a would-be champion show jumper who will never get to the top through lack of cash in buying really first class horse-flesh, might be a lot happier learning the pleasures of all round horsemanship – dressage, cross country and show jumping – in the field of combined training. Perhaps the boom in combined training nowadays is partly because many youngsters ARE making this discovery.

One encouraging sign for the future of show jumping is that despite the austere economic scene there is still a considerable amount of sponsorship available. In 1970 some £180,000 was offered in prize money at jumping competitions, much of it provided by sponsors. Other sponsors, such as Ford of Britain, gave help in kind. Ford gave the B.S.J.A. two horse boxes, a luggage van and a bus, and presented three new Cortinas as prizes at the Horse of the Year Show.

Despite this outside help the B.S.J.A. itself will have to watch its finances carefully in future, even though it is holding its own.

Before the 1971 season got under way Sir Mike Ansell warned: "We have the possibility of tax problems looming. I hope and believe any tax authority will treat this Association as generously as possible within the law.

"We do two great jobs for the country. First, we beat the foreigner and so raise our national prestige. Secondly, at the present time in the world there is much militancy, and recently I was interested to read and learn about what is termed 'risk sport'.

"In years gone by there were wars, and for those wanting excitement almost permanent active service. Today a substitute must be provided by something which involves a risk. This may be climbing a mountain, canoeing round the coast, or riding.

"We, I hope, provide the opportunity to get excitement and take a risk. The other alternative is perhaps marching to some Embassy and slinging a brick. It would seem better for the tax authorities to be generous to the show jumper!"

40

WORLD CHAMPION

DAVID BROOME

Only the winning of an Olympic gold medal now eludes David Broome in his fabulous career in the show jumping ring. He says his biggest disappointment was being a member of two British teams which were eliminated in the Olympic Games.

At Rome in 1960 three refusals by Franco, ridden by David Barker, sank Britain's hopes of a team victory, and at Mexico Stroller's fall and elimination had the same effect in '68.

Yet 30 is no great age for a show jumping rider, and David has two individual bronze Olympic medals, won with Sunsalve at Rome and with Mister Softee at the Mexico Games.

Even if '72 should not be Britain's year, and David is *not* confident of major placings at Munich, with good luck he still has plenty of time to achieve the ultimate honour of an Olympic gold.

His European championship victory in '69 with Mister Softee at Hickstead rightly earned him immense praise throughout the show jumping world.

Yet his 1970 triumph in winning the world championship at La Baule in France eclipsed the big win of the previous year. The world championship proved to be an effective test of sheer horsemanship, and David passed this test so brilliantly.

How down in the mouth were the "experts" when it was announced that John Massarella, owner of Mister Softee, was not providing him for David to ride in the world championship.

The respected show jumping correspondent of *The Times* announced flatly that "Britain's chance of winning a men's world show jumping championship . . . evaporated" with the news that David had lost the ride on Mister Softee. It appeared Mr Massarella wanted the horse to be ridden at local shows in the north.

David Broome admitted the decision was "a shock" but did not commit himself publicly to the general theme of gloom and doom being purveyed by some equestrian writers. Britain's chances of winning "plummeted from hot favourite to near bottom", said the *Daily Express*.

On paper, the form of the contending horses certainly did not give Britain much chance of victory. Yet it now seems most observers under-estimated the importance of the final round in the men's championship where the riders compete on each of their rival's horses. True, one had to do well in earlier rounds to reach the final, but David and Harvey Smith soon set about showing they could do this.

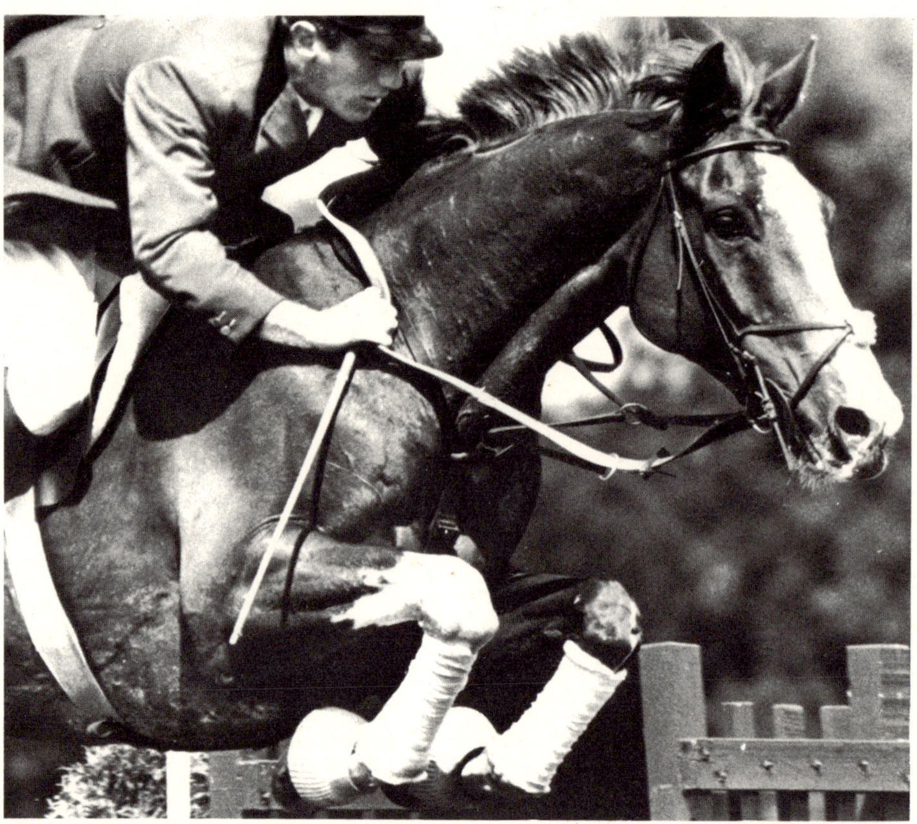

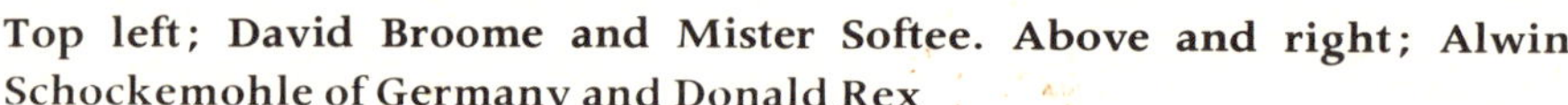

Top left; David Broome and Mister Softee. Above and right; Alwin Schockemohle of Germany and Donald Rex

Douglas Bunn, after early successes having had a disappointing patch with his rather truculent black horse, Beethoven, is much to be congratulated on having made him available carte blanche to David Broome.

David's skill in handling a difficult horse enabled him to form a remarkable partnership with Beethoven, sired by Roi d'Egypte out of an Irish draught mare. Tail-swishing exuberance and a tendency to kick-back had already marked down Beethoven as a ''character'' long before he strode into show jumping history at La Baule.

With hindsight, it is possible to see Beethoven as a brilliant choice for the world championship, since his ebullience, or cussedness if you prefer it, would be likely to make him a less than easy ride for the other riders in the final ''change-over'' round.

Harvey Smith, on form, had a better chance with Mattie Brown, since this horse has the all round capability for speed and puissance so vital in the world championship. Mattie Brown demonstrated his quality by winning the first qualifying round, designed to test speed. Alwin Schockemohle with the great Donald Rex was runner-up, and retained his position as hot favourite for the championship. David Broome, though troubled by an upset stomach, brought Beethoven into third place.

The next round was a puissance (high jumping) event over an eight fence course which included a true parallel, 4 feet 9 inches high with a 5 feet 9 inches spread. Mattie Brown jumped clear twice to give Harvey Smith another superb victory, with Hugo Arrambide of Argentina and Adagio in second place. Third was Graziano Mancinelli with Fidux, the horse most likely to provide too exciting a ride for other riders in the final. Fidux has a well known reputation as a "dog", which considering most horsemen like dogs, is nevertheless the term they apply to a horse which can be a brute to ride.

After this second round, Harvey was in overall leading position, but David and Beethoven had not had such a successful second round and were in overall seventh position. They redeemed themselves in the third round, over a big Nations Cup type course, winning with two clear rounds.

This qualified both Harvey and David to ride in the four-man final, the first time two riders from one country had ever achieved this. The other two finalists were Alwin Schockemohle with Donald Rex and Mancinelli with Fidux. It was a fascinating combination indeed, certainly one of the most interesting encounters in show jumping history.

Of the four finalists, Schockemohle's Donald Rex was rated the best; Mancinelli's Fidux the worse. Yet this was likely to be a disadvantage to Schockemohle since it meant the disciplined, obedient Donald Rex would probably provide the easiest ride for the other competitors in the final, whereas Fidux would probably be the most intractable.

David's performance with Fidux proved to be the key to his victory. In the first of the four rounds in the final, when each man rode his own horse, only Harvey Smith and Mattie Brown disappointingly failed to go clear, having five faults. There were clear seconds rounds by Mancinelli, now riding Donald Rex and David Broome with Mattie Brown. But Schockemohle had four faults riding Beethoven. Harvey Smith jumped well to pick up only four faults with Fidux who nearly took him into an unused water jump, had to be pulled up quickly, and then struck the first part of the treble.

Thus at the start of the crucial third round, only David Broome and Graziano Mancinelli, had gone entirely clear so far.

Dorian Williams, commentating on BBC television from La Baule, provided these words to the pictures as the contest became more taut and exciting every minute:

"Mancinelli is now on the difficult Beethoven of David Broome . . . only David and Mancinelli are clear at this stage and David will be next in . . . very active rider, Mancinelli, matching the very active Beethoven with his swishing tail . . . comes into the big treble . . . hurtles into it . . . Mancinelli, having the sense not to get him sharply round the corner . . . because he's still clear and now he approaches the water . . . fifteen feet of water . . . and he's right in it . . . four faults at the water.

"Now David Broome on Mancinelli's Fidux, the notoriously difficult horse to ride . . . can he make it three clear rounds over

David Broome and Beethoven, his World Championship partner

this very difficult ten fence course? . . .
seems to have got Fidux properly settled . . .
going remarkably kindly for him . . . he
jumps that well . . . I've seldom seen Fidux
go more kindly . . . now the big treble . . .
absolutely flew it . . . still clear as he goes
into the last of the ten jumps, the fifteen feet
of water . . . (gasps and oohs from the
crowd) . . . and he stood right back to get
over it . . . right back at the water there . . .
must have jumped at least eighteen feet to
clear the water . . . a tremendous jump to give
him a clear round . . . so David is clear . . .
Mancinelli has four faults . . . Harvey Smith
nine and three quarters . . . Schockemohle
twelve.''

As Dorian had discerned instantly, David
Broome had the skill and the intuitive under-
standing to master the hard-pulling German-
bred Fidux quickly, and conjured a clear
round out of him. Beethoven, difficult in his

own way, had not responded so sympatheti-
cally to Mancinelli's style which can be
effective in its rugged forcefulness, but has
none of the subtlety of David Broome's free
riding methods.

In the final round, as Dorian Williams reported, the ''erratic and dramatic'' Mancinelli had Mattie Brown going well for him,
but again made a mistake at the end.
Dorian's commentary described it thus . . .
''still clear as he turns to the water . . .
going very wide as he turns . . . zig-zagging
into it . . . yes, at the take-off, a hand has
gone up . . . four faults at the water, giving
Mancinelli a final total of eight faults''.

The excitement was tremendous as David
came in for his fourth round – anything less
than eight faults and he would win the
championship. His mount: Schockemohle's
Donald Rex. It was the first time he had
ridden a German horse, and quite a few

knuckles whitened among the British contingent as David set out to attempt his fourth clear round.

Dorian's television commentary as David began his round: "In the opinion of many people this Donald Rex is the greatest show jumper in the world . . . Hanoverian bred . . . already they seem to be in complete harmony . . . David is very quickly adapting himself to the Germanic style of riding, the very different style . . . now coming into the treble . . . he's wrong . . . yes the third part has gone . . . now, he can't afford another mistake, and there're just two jumps to go . . . turning very short into the water . . . accelerating in a few strides . . . and again he's done it . . . a prodigious jump! a prodigious jump! . . . and so he's done it! He's the new world champion!"

David Broome said afterwards his problem at the treble had been that the big German horse failed to accelerate when "let go" in the manner of the horses David usually rides. Yet it was Donald Rex's only mistake throughout the championship final, and surprisingly Fidux was second with only two fences down, Beethoven had 12 faults and Mattie Brown had 17.

Graziano Mancinelli was runner-up in the championship, with Harvey Smith adding more lustre for Britain by finishing third, and Alwin Schockemohle fourth.

Although not to everyone's taste, one had to concede the effectiveness of the changeover method in the world championship in exploring the prowess of each rider. David Broome was the first Briton to win the championship since it began in 1953. It's likely to be a hard task to wrest it from him when he is called upon to defend his title.

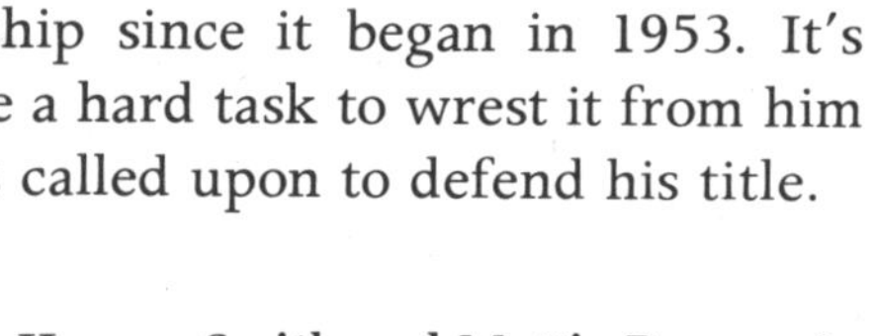

Harvey Smith and Mattie Brown ▶

CANADA CALLING

It wasn't a fluke! It wasn't a fluke! It wasn't a fluke! Yes, they will keep saying it in Canada, and who can blame them.

This was the forthright reaction of Canadian team members and their supporters to the reaction of some observers in Britain and elsewhere, when Canada won the team gold medal in the '68 Mexico Olympic Games.

The Canadians have proved their point, and reiterated that it simply wasn't a fluke, by following up with more notable victories.

They beat the Americans by taking the top four places in the United States – Canada Grand Prix clash in June, 1969.

There have been plenty of other wins by the Canadians to answer the criticism from some equestrian writers that their Mexico achievement was aided by luck.

The Canadians are determined to prove at Munich in '72 they are still capable of defending their Olympic gold medals.

We had a chance to see them in action in Britain last year, and apart from admiring their undoubted skill it was a great pleasure to meet these Canadian riders, four very pleasant guys and a charming girl.

Barbara Simpson, from Calgary, Alberta, has notched up some wonderful performances on her 11-years-old bay mare, Australis, and both are as well known in Europe as in Canada.

Jim Day, Jim Elder, and Tom Gayford were all members of the Olympic gold medal winning team, and the fifth team member, John Moffat Dunlap, was Olympic reserve rider.

In contrast to most of the "amateur" riders of Britain and other European countries, the Canadians all have busy full time jobs outside the world of horses. Jim Day is a car salesman, Jim Elder is a refrigerator distributor, Tom Gayford a stock broker, and John Dunlap sells real estate.

Like the Australians who visited Britain the previous year, the Canadians are extremely approachable and prepared to talk about their sport with the enthusiasm of someone who does it for fun.

This is another contrast to certain leading British riders who tend to get a wary look in the eye if asked to express an opinion on anything except the weather, and hungrily expect a fee if asked to say anything "on the record". I would emphasise this only applies to a few, and to be charitable one cannot blame people in a highly expensive sport such as show jumping trying to augment their incomes. Alas, in some cases, the brusque, business-like comments which some of these U.K. riders make when they do allow themselves to talk about their sport, give a strong impression that for them much of the fun was lost on the way to the top.

Jim Elder, intended to ride The Immigrant and Pieces of Eight, on the European tour, but because of injuries had to compete on two lesser known horses, Shoeman and Beefeater.

Other Canadian team horses suffered fitness problems, yet the team did remarkably well at the start of their tour, winning the team event at La Baule.

"Shoeman surprised me at La Baule", Jim Elder told me afterwards. "It was a very big course, and he seemed to cope with the big fences as well as any horse there. He's only an eight year old, and I'm very pleased with him.

"Fortunately The Immigrant, which I rode in Mexico, is only nine and he has been jumping fantastically since then, but I think Shoeman could be a useful prospect for Munich in '72 as well.

"Up to about five years ago, a lot of good young Canadian horses were sold to the United States for a lot of money, but nowadays we hang on to these horses, and we spend a lot of time developing them. I don't think we have such an intensive season as your show jumpers seem to have in Britain. We only go to ten or 15 big shows in a year, and mostly they are just one day shows at a weekend, with perhaps four or five shows during the year which are two or more days.

"I think this regime has probably benefited our horses, but it's always nice to see what the opposition does elsewhere."

I asked Jim Elder about the surprise in international show jumping over the Canadians' sudden leap to prominence with their Olympic win.

"I guess you have to say you are surprised to some extent when you come up with a big win", he replied with a smile. But mainly the reason why people did not rate us beforehand was because they had never seen us. The big league of show jumping is mainly in Europe and we had to be content to train in our own back yard, but we did use big, solid Olympic type courses, so that when we did get to Mexico, the course did not surprise us. We knew it would be big — and it certainly was. Still, we didn't think: Oh gee, I'll never make that jump.

"Looking ahead to Munich in '72, barring further injury, we should still have the three horses that we had in '68. We shall also be bringing on some younger horses, so that we should have a little more 'depth' in our team, with good horses as reserves to fill the places of any of our best horses if they should become unfit through injury.

"I think therefore, we have equally as good a chance as we did in 1968, perhaps even a little better."

Seven or eight of the horses brought to Europe by the Canadians were on the injury list early during their tour. For this reason, none of the horses they had used at La Baule, competed at Wembley when they

Barbara Simpson of Canada and Australis

finished third in the Nations Cup event behind Italy second, and Britain in first place. Anyone who judged the Canadians by their Wembley performance should bear this in mind.

Jim Day's best horses, Canadian Club and Steelmaster, suffered tendon troubles and cuts jumping at La Baule and at Hickstead. One of Jim Elder's horses suffered a bruised foot. These are inevitable perils in show jumping, and when a team is travelling a long way from home it is not possible suddenly to call on reserves.

Although the Canadian riders are certainly amateurs in the true sense of the word, they demonstrate clearly their will to win. Jim Elder remarked with a grin that they are "just as interested in prize money" as anyone else, and he thought the level of prize money on the North American circuit was "reasonable".

"If you take our international circuit in the fall – Harrisburg, New York, Washington, and Toronto – there is nearly 50,000 dollars there in prize money, just for the international teams."

(Compare this with, say, the Prince of Wales Cup at the Royal International Horse Show in London, where the winning team simply receives a challenge cup and trophies. Thus, to win big prize money, our top jumpers must compete in many individual events other than international team events.)

The Canadian team horses are all owned privately, some belonging to the riders and some to other people prepared to support the team – the same basis on which the British teams are founded.

Douglas J. Cudney, of Burlington, Ontario, is chairman of the Canadian Equestrian Jumping team, and formerly rode in the team for eight years. He undoubtedly has

Jim Day and Canadian Club ▲

▼ **Jim Elder and The Immigrant,**

a dynamic approach to making his country's team successful.

When I met the Canadian team, Mr Cudney was planning for the Pan American Games this year, the next Olympics, and the Olympics in '76.

He had the excellent idea of forming a panel of professional horsemen on an advisory basis to pool their experience and ability on behalf of the team.

"They are closer to developing young talent in both horses and riders than anyone else, and we will need their help to give the team depth", said Mr Cudney. "I also plan to include our top junior talent in several competitions each year with our senior team, to give them the experience of top level competition. Pony Club and Junior International riders are the source of our future team members, and we hope to tap this resource to the utmost."

From London, the Canadian team went to Dublin where they finished fourth in the Nations Cup contest, in which there were six teams competing. So the Canadians' first European tour for 16 years ended with just one Nations Cup triumph, that at La Baule, to their credit. They had reinforced old contacts and made many new friends. Everyone felt they should not wait another 16 years to return to Britain. The Germans dominated the New York show at the end of 1970, winning the Nations Cup in which the Canadians were in fifth, and final, position. But of the team which had earlier toured Europe, only Barbara Simpson was competing in the Canadian contingent in New York.

Do not be surprised if Messrs Gayford, Elder and Day "surprise" us again at Munich. Whatever happens it won't be a fluke.

WORLD CHAMPION

JANOU LEFEBVRE

In the season when Britain gained the men's world championship, we lost the ladies' title.

Yet there was not an atom of disgrace in the latter, since British girls, Marion Mould and Anneli Drummond-Hay, filled second and third places.

It was indeed a remarkable performance by Marion – formerly Marion Coakes, of course, before her marriage to steeplechase rider David Mould – to secure a silver medal with the same brilliant mount with which she had won the world title five years earlier.

The incredible Stroller came so close to retaining the championship for Marion, and there is every reason to believe he would have done so if there had been a chance of a day's rest before the final round of the contest.

Although it was little known, and unpublished at the time, Marion tells me her amazing 14·2 hands pony had a recurrence of the sinus trouble which had affected him so adversely during the Mexico Olympic Games. This second attack was not so serious, being unaccompanied by the septic tooth from which he had suffered before, but it put his form a little below par. Marion thinks the dryness of the ladies' championship course at Copenhagen, with a lot of dust blowing about, had something to do with Stroller's trouble.

Yet the champion, who emerged after the three gruelling rounds of the contest, France's attractive Janou Lefebvre, certainly deserved her victory.

Janou, aged 25, from Aix-en-Provence, has two Olympic team silver medals. She was the youngest ever Olympic rider when she competed at the Tokyo Games, riding Kenavo D, a superb horse by the French sire Foudroyant. They finished 14th in the individual event at Tokyo. Rocket, formerly a racehorse, proved a superb successor as a mount for Janou. They were third in the European championships, and the same year helped France take the team silver medal at the Mexico Olympics, gaining the best score in the French team.

Janou has been known to "go to pieces" somewhat on a big occasion, affecting her concentration while jumping, but she seems to have conquered this handicap, and at Copenhagen she rode with great determination and verve throughout. Rocket had been carefully prepared with the championship in mind, avoiding the "summer circuit" of intensive jumping in which some of his rivals had been engaged as usual.

The first round was a speed event over a

15 fence course. Janou, Marion, and Anneli riding Merely-a-Monarch, went clear, but the French girl had the best time and took first place.

Stroller showed his prowess next day, winning the second qualifier, over a stiff Nations Cup type course. Runners-up were Anneli and Brazil's Lucia Faria with Rush du Camp.

The final contest was a two round event, over 18 fences the first time, and 12 the second. They were formidable fences in the second round, some being well over five feet.

Janou and Marion shared the overall lead at this stage, with Anneli third.

Anneli's brilliant Merely-a-Monarch went clear in the first round over the long, tiring course, and a British victory seemed possible – a very popular victory too. The big, dark bay has a special place in the affections of both horse trials' and show jumping supporters, since he is one of the rare horses to excel at both, having won at Badminton.

Eliza Perez de las Heras during the Imperial Cup at the Royal International Horse Show

Janou and Rocket had one fence down in the first round, a parallel, and Stroller had two down. Eliza Perez de las Heras and Eleonora, from Mexico, only had one fence down in this first round. Many British TV

Janou Lefebvre and Rocket

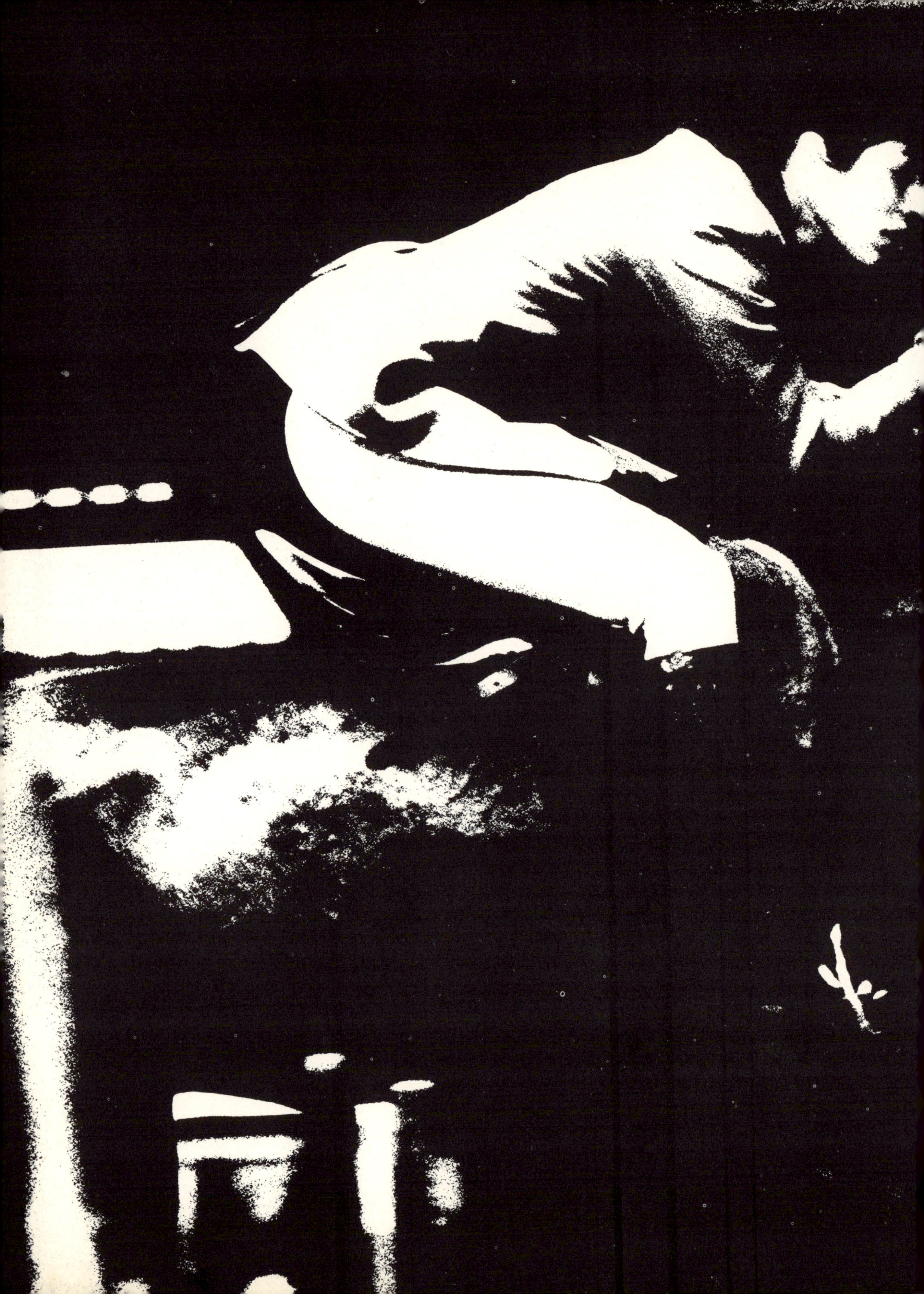

Janou Lefebvre during the ''Martell''
International Invitation Championships
at Upminster

Lucia Faria of Brazil and Rush du Camp

Ann Moore and Psalm

viewers will recall their shattering fall in the second round of the John Player Trophy at the Royal International Horse Show. Yet Eleonora has proved herself a first class mare, and may do well at Munich.

In the second round of the final at Copenhagen, it appeared the veteran Merely-a-Monarch shared Stroller's view that 12 more fences are rather too many after such a gruelling first round over 18 obstacles. Monarch put in a stop at the seventh fence, and then hit the oxer which followed, but Anneli finished with just half a time fault.

The excellent Eleonora provided a superb clear round; a pity she had not risen to this form earlier in the contest, for the title might easily have gone to Mexico.

Stroller started well on the last round, but Marion said afterwards he seemed rather tired, and he could not manage the big treble combination, bringing all three elements down. When the accurate Stroller does such a thing, there must be something wrong.

Janou's chance was plain, and she took it convincingly, jumping a fluent clear round with Rocket, and not being tempted to hurry too much they finished with just half a time fault.

On over-all totals, Marion and Anneli had equal marks, but Marion was placed second because she had won the event on the second day.

If she has the right mount at the time, one would like to see 20-years-old Ann Moore included in a future British team in the championship. She filled reserve place in the team at Copenhagen and won first and third places with Psalm and April Love in the opening event, in which all the world contenders competed, but which did not count towards the championship.

Britain has more girls in show jumping than men, and it was to be hoped the 1971 European championships at St Gall, Switzerland, would bring forth a young British girl rider who will go forward to new international stardom in the tradition of Pat Smythe and Marion Mould.

STONELEIGH

During 1971 Dorian Williams was completing his term as Honorary Director of the most exciting post war project in the horse world – the National Equestrian Centre at Stoneleigh, Warwickshire.

It's the one place in Britain where horsemen break out of their compartments – show jumping, horse trials, dressage and other activities. They work together with the common bond of horsemanship in all its aspects, sharing a desire to learn more of this vast and fascinating subject, thereby helping to raise standards throughout Britain.

As always, some tried to pour cold water on a new idea. The splendid progress made under Dorian Williams' leadership has more than answered the critics since the Centre was opened by Princess Anne in April, 1969.

Its aim was to provide a national "equestrian university" – a centre with facilities for training instructors, for riders who may be chosen to represent the country in equestrian sport, and for holding courses and conferences.

As well as these worthy activities, all booming, Stoneleigh has had a big share in the glamour of television show jumping. The steeple chase jockey's television events, and novelties such as the relay speed events over fences, have become widely popular with the enormous television public already wedded to the thrills of the Royal International and the Horse of the Year shows.

Some people inside the horse world have sniffed at Stoneleigh's "show biz" role. Is this really what it was meant for, they ask? The fact is that television fees have played a valuable part in helping to make Stoneleigh a financial success.

Dorian, who will remain as chairman of the management committee after handing on the Director's post, replies: "Apart from the value and entertainment of the competitions themselves, the fact that millions of viewers are watching means that more and more people are learning of the National Equestrian Centre and taking an interest in it."

They expected an annual loss for the first three years of the N.E.C. yet it was making a profit at the end of its second year. No other sport would expect its national training centre to make a profit at any time! It would simply be a case of asking for government subsidies and private patronage indefinitely.

The regular clinics held at the Centre are all over-subscribed. Riders take their horses to Stoneleigh, and each one has an individual lesson and advice in the superb indoor riding school from a leading expert in a specialised field of horsemanship. For example, Peter Robeson has been coaching young show jumpers.

The site of the N.E.C. was a parcel of land offered by the Royal Agricultural Society on their showground at the Agricultural Centre, Stoneleigh. Three hundred founder members of the Equestrian Centre donated a hundred guineas each, this £30,000 was brought up to the final £70,000 needed by loans from the B.S.J.A. and the British Horse Society, the sale of the lease of their London headquarters, and a Government grant.

The two organisations now have joint headquarters in the new office block at Stoneleigh, which was followed by the construction of the 100 feet by 200 feet indoor riding school, the most modern and fully equipped in Britain, possibly the most advanced in the world.

Entering the school through the main doors one is faced with a ground floor gallery of showcases displaying goods of interest to horsemen and women, and the Centre's information bureau where all details of courses and accommodation can be obtained.

The ring itself is big enough for a full sized course of 12 jumps; it is slightly larger than the ring at the Empire Pool, Wembley. It is surfaced with sand and wood shavings, slightly salted to retain moisture. Overhead is a plastics roof which allows a diffused, shadowless light through to the ring.

A 400-seat gallery runs the length of the ring, many of the tip-up seats having been contributed by Pony Club branches from all over the world, who have their names attached to the seats. Horse breeding societies have taken an area of the panel under the gallery for a display of pictures of their specific breeds, and the Hunts of Britain have taken glass panels in the arcade with their names on them. The money received for these areas and panels helped to pay for much of the school's equipment.

At one end of the gallery there is a canteen, and at the other end of the building a conference room overlooks the ring through large picture windows. Leading off this room is a library, and on the ground floor is a lecture room and first aid or rest room.

During instruction in the ring pupils and instructors are able to communicate through a two-way microphone system, whereby the instructor talks to the rider through a microphone, and the rider hears the message on a transistor receiver in his top pocket.

Plans for more development are most ambitious. The next priority is to build the Centre's own stabling for visiting horses and ponies. It is intended to build another gallery at one end of the riding school to accommodate 250 more spectators.

Although delayed by legal difficulties over the use of land, the N.E.C. has plans well in hand for a full size cross country course some two miles long. It will include a set of four or five different courses, designed to suit riders of varying experience. Here riders may train over 30 to 40 schooling fences for cross-country competitions, on courses graded up to the standard of three day events. Pony and Riding Club events are held on a course already built on this land

Next to the indoor school is a large grassed arena suitable for a show of international calibre, this and the main arena in front of the Centre's offices will be available for competitions and demonstrations on dates other than those occupied by the Royal Show. Later it is hoped to build a permanent jumping course on a five-acre field near the cross-country course, and there are plans for outdoor manege areas for schooling.

Much accomplished – yet much to be done. Thus the N.E.C. offers an exciting future for British riders and horse enthusiasts of all ages and experience. Owing to the post war boom in riding as a leisure activity, there has never been such a need for qualified instructors in Britain and the N.E.C. is playing a vital role in training them. Stable manager is a less well known career with horses, but it is becoming increasingly important, and the N.E.C. gives valuable training in this field.

Dorian Williams tells me one scheme he wants to see tackled urgently is a scholarship system so that keen, young riders who cannot afford to pay fees can still gain top class instruction in Stoneleigh.

"It's the sort of thing a Centre such as ours should be doing", says Dorian. "I would like to see, as a start, about six or eight grants of £1,000 a year each for this project."

Next time you see televised show jumping from Stoneleigh, remember there is much more going on there during the day, and Stoneleigh welcomes visitors.

Dorian says: "Visitors are essential to the success of the school. The fees paid by those attending a course barely cover the expenses. The school will only make ends meet if there are, in addition to those taking part, visitors watching."

Sitting-in on one of Stoneleigh's training sessions is an entertainment – and an education. Even if you cannot take your own horse to Stoneleigh you will learn much from the gallery.

One of the happiest aspects of the Stoneleigh idea is that one of the main beneficiaries is certain to be – the horse. The versatility of the horse is immense – he provides sport and entertainment of so many kinds – and treated properly he is the kindest and most generous of animals. Yet one by-product of the riding boom has been the increase in horse keeping by those who mean well, but know very little about the subject. Even more than a pet dog, a horse or pony can be killed or made miserable by kindness unaccompanied by knowledge.

Cruelty can be stamped out by watchfulness and legislation. Misery just this side of cruelty is less difficult to erase. By providing a new generation of better instructors and stable managers, Stoneleigh will be doing a great service to the British horseman – and to his best friend.

The arenas at famous Horse Shows of the past . . . top left; The International Horse Show Olympia, on Kings Day, 1909. Top right; More jumping contests in 1909; and below, The jumps at The Agricultural Hall, 1871

IT SHOWS IN YOUR FACE

Brian Mullins

ELEVATION, DAMNATION, DETERMINATION,

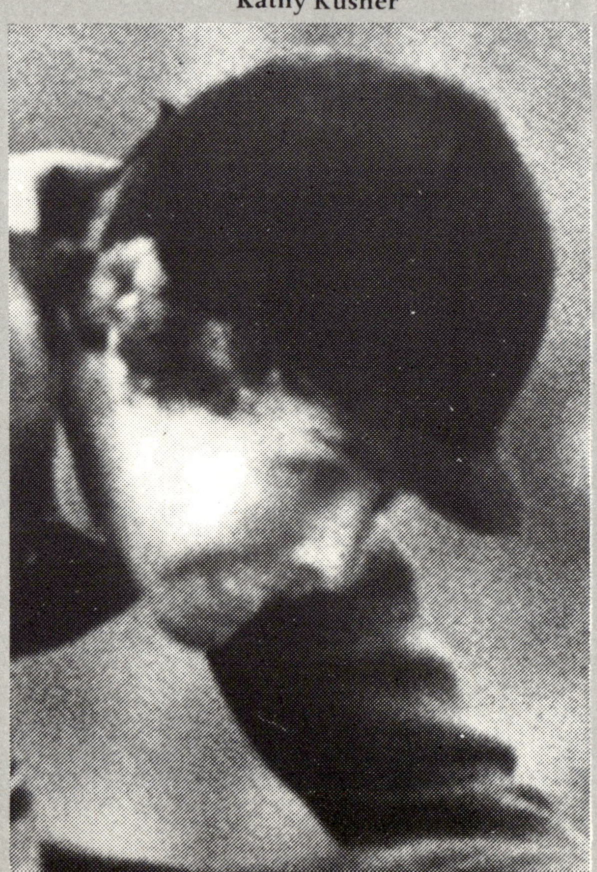

Kathy Kusner

Capt. Fernando Hernandez I

Carol Hoffman

Anneli Drummond-Hay

HESITATION, CONCENTRATION, ANTICIPATION

Alison Westwood

Hans Winkler

ANOTHER GOLD FOR BRITAIN?

If I had to place a bet on an Olympic event in which Britain stood the best chance of a medal in 1972, I would unhesitatingly choose the horse trials.

Yet so many disasters can so easily befall a three day event team long before they compete, that I would still expect fairly long odds for my bet.

After their Mexico victory, and their 1970 world championship win, Britain *must* be favourites for the gold at Munich. On paper we have a better chance of winning the three day event medals than the show jumping medals.

The hazardous nature of eventing's cross-country phase increases the chances of injury to such an extent that success in international horse trials must depend to a great extent on the calibre of reserve horses available in an emergency.

We were able to produce a brilliant "emergency" horse (Cornishman) in Mexico, and at this stage there seem to be plenty of good British horses to be considered candidates for the '72 Olympics. There is no dearth of superb young British event riders either, and we are fortunate in having some of the most experienced advisers in the world in coaching event teams, and in veterinary skills to keep our horses fit for competition. The latter is a vital factor – never more so than at the high altitude in Mexico

when considerable forethought and planning by veterinary surgeon Peter Scott-Dunn was undoubtedly a major factor in producing horses which could win under appalling conditions.

Who can forget the sudden flood which rendered the cross country course almost lethal, adding to the respiratory and feeding difficulties already posed by the location?

West Germany should be free of such bizarre hazards; the Germans deservedly have a reputation for good organisation, and the climate will provide no special problems for our horses. This will apply to most of our rivals, and their competition may be much more potent than in Mexico. Yet the unexpected can so easily upset all the horse trials form books.

Britain performed true to form in winning the world championship at Punchestown in Ireland last autumn, but the event can hardly be said to have been without surprises.

The Irish organisers were soundly castigated for alleged bad organisation. The cross country course was bitterly criticised for poor construction and design. There were 46 falls on the course by the 36 horses still

Richard Meade and The Poacher ▶

Richard Meade and The Poacher during obstacle 21/22/23 at the World Championship 3-day event

competing, and by the end of it 19 were either eliminated or retired.

In fairness to the organisers, one must report that the cross-country was held in a heavy downpour of rain, but there were also criticisms of the poor control of the crowds of spectators who were sometimes a hindrance to competitors, sometimes a danger.

All these hazards add even more to the achievement of Britain's Mary Gordon-Watson and the superb Cornishman V in winning the individual world championship, and playing their part in the British team victory as well.

Already holder of the European title, Mary is one of the most delightful personalities at the top of Britain's horse world. At 22, her slim, blonde good looks are far from the conventional picture of an English "horsey" female. Yet Mary, while maintaining her femininity, demonstrates impressive strength of mind and body in meeting the enormous challenge of international three day events. The dangers are real indeed, and the strict rules debarring women from competing in Olympic three day events were only relaxed at Tokyo in 1964 when the first woman to take part was Mrs Helen du Pont of the United States.

Jane Bullen's role as the first British girl to compete in the three day Olympics – riding Our Nobby in Mexico – must surely be followed in 1972 by Mary Gordon-Watson's participation, unless some malignant fate attacks Cornishman.

By 1972 this magnificent bay, a seven-eighths thoroughbred by the premium stallion Golden Surprise, will only be twelve years old, and barring accidents at the peak of his form.

66

As the late entry in the British team in Mexico he gave Richard Meade a wonderfully safe ride over the flooded course, and since then this "horse of a lifetime" has continued to show his brilliance with Mary in the saddle.

Understandably, Cornishman is no longer risked in the hunting field, although he is the ideal mount every hunting man or woman would wish to ride after hounds. Yet in the Portman country in North Dorset, Mary is often to be seen in the winter months, riding young horses across the grass vale with its big thorn hedges, guarded by wide ditches.

Mary lives in the Portman's hill country and has to drive to the vale, so I was amused when an inhabitant of the vale asked me: "Who *is* that attractive girl? I'm sure I've seen her somewhere before. She certainly seems to know how to cross country."

"She should", I replied. "She's the world champion event rider – and she's just been elected Sportswoman of the Year by the British Sports Writers' Association."

Assuming Cornishman is fit and going as well as ever, which must mean his automatic inclusion in the team, who else will accompany him to West Germany?

Of the 1968 winning team, Richard Meade is the one member almost certain to compete in Olympics again. He had some brilliant successes last year, riding The Poacher who was of course the Mexico Olympics partner of Staff Sergeant Ben Jones. Richard and The Poacher won the 1970 Badminton event when only 17 of the 43 starters jumped the formidable cross country course clear.

At Punchestown The Poacher and Richard Meade were runners-up in the in-

▼ **Left to Right: The Great Britain winning team: Richard Meade, Mark Phillips, Tom Durston-Smith and Mary Gordon-Watson**

▲ The Great Britain Team lined up at Punchestown
Lorna Sutherland and Popadom ▼

dividual event, and aided Britain's team victory, but they had a nasty fall at fence 29, a 6ft oxer off a bank with a big drop. Meade had to ride with his shoulder strapped up in the final phase, the show jumping round, but they jumped this clear to gain their world championship silver medal.

The Poacher, 14-years-old, was in his last season in international trials and was enjoying himself in the hunting field thereafter.

Meade's mount for West Germany, if selected, would therefore probably be the splendid grey Flamingo, which belongs to those notable patrons of eventing, Lord and Lady Hugh Russell who run the excellent Wylye event at their Wiltshire home.

Mark Phillips, the other member of the British team at Punchestown to complete the event, could well be a likely candidate for West Germany with his world championship mount, Chicago III, owned by Bertie Hill. Mark's earlier successes were all with the well known Rock On, but this excellent horse was no longer fit for top eventing, so Mark's candidature for the next Olympics depends on the availability of Chicago III or some other horse of similar calibre.

It would undoubtedly bring a great deal of pleasure to many three day event enthusiasts if Lorna Sutherland should find a place in a British Olympic team. Lorna, from the north of Scotland, makes impressive sorties into the English eventing scene each season with the eye catching skewbald horses, Gypsy Flame and Popadom.

At Badminton last year she performed the extraordinary feat of riding three horses in the event, and finishing with all three — Gypsy Flame in fourth place, Popadom

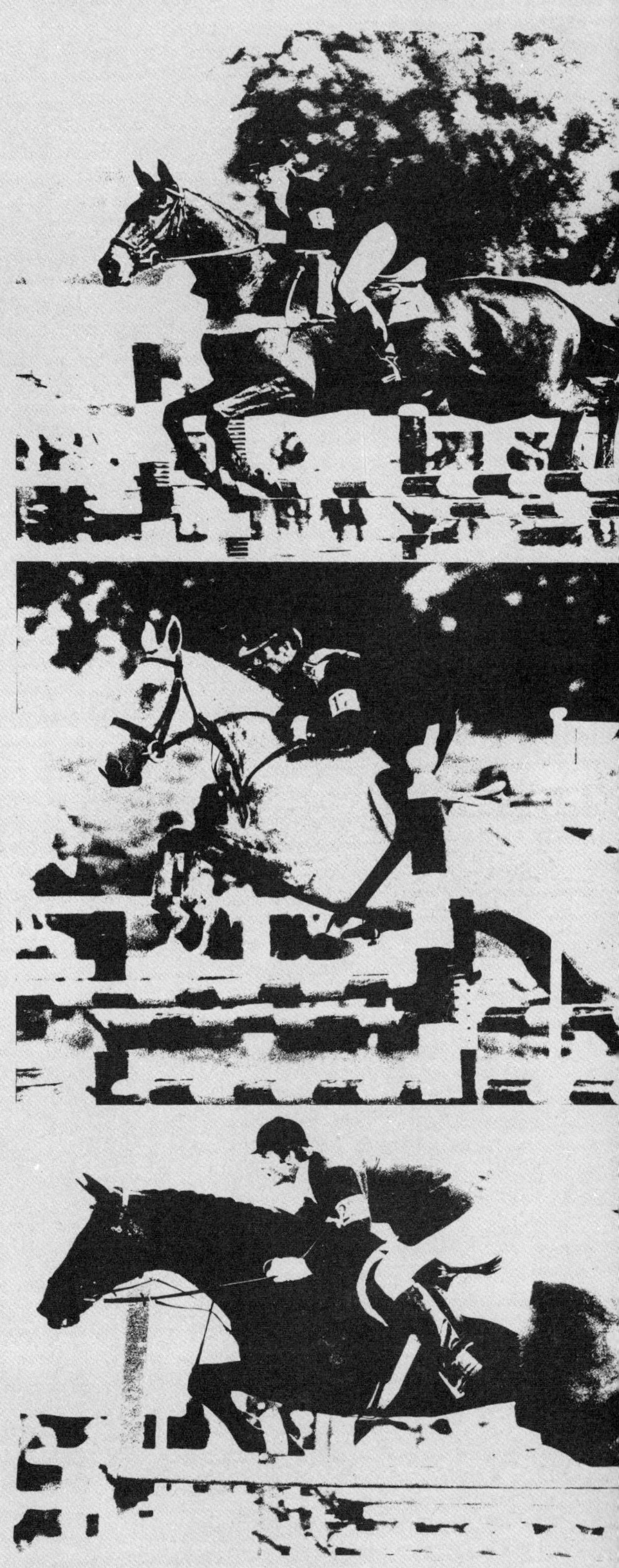

Mary Gordon-Watson and Cornishman
Mark Phillips and Cargo
Richard Meade and The Poacher

The Great Britain team. L-R; Richard Meade, Lt. Mark Phillips, Tom Durston-Smith, Mary Gordon-Watson and Chief D'Equipe Lt. Col. W. S. P. Lithgow

twelfth, and The Dark Horse fifteenth. It entailed riding 50 miles during the cross country day and jumping 132 fences.

If courage, endurance and skill are necessary attributes for an Olympic rider then Lorna has proved on many occasions that she has all three. A possible Olympic mount for her could be Major Derek Allhusen's Laurieston, with which Lorna won an Intermediate class at Wylye last year. Laurieston is out of Laurien, the mare which Allhusen used to ride with great success in international events, and the sire was Happy Monarch, whose progeny include Anneli Drummond-Hay's famous eventer and show jumper Merely-a-Monarch. With such an eminent background, one is justified in hoping for great things from Laurieston and perhaps by the autumn of 1972 we shall have had further evidence of a great new eventing partnership.

The Dutch three day event at Deurne, right at the end of the 1970 season, gave Olympic selectors plenty to think about. The winner was a new winning British pair: Michael Moffett and Demerara, who secured victory by virtue of a splendid performance on the exceptionally formidable cross country course. Lorna Sutherland, with Peer Gynt, were in second place, and Richard Meade came third with Flamingo.

It could yet be that some name I have not mentioned will blazon forth in Olympic honours for Britain in '72, but in horse trials plans have to be made well ahead and time runs out fast for the selectors who have to make a realistic short list long in advance of the Games. One hopes owners of some of Britain's best event horses are able to resist the inevitable offers from overseas buyers.

Unless calamity strikes, there must be more horse trials Olympic medals for Britain. I'm even willing to place a modest bet on our chances of striking gold again.

Lorna Sutherland with her three mounts, L-R; Dark Horse, Popadom and Gypsy Flame

Mark Phillips and Chicago ploughing through the
water to jump the fence at Punchestown

HORSE TRIALS STILL LEAPING AHEAD

Britain's prowess in three day eventing on the international scene reflects the tremendous boom in this sport at home.

Fleet Street has hardly woken up to it, since even some of the "quality" papers still run brief reports on eventing under the overall heading of "Show Jumping".

Yet there is no doubt plenty of awareness of eventing's growing importance in some quarters where it matters, since the sport is benefiting still more each season from increased sponsorship from banking and industry.

Offering a challenge in dressage, cross country riding, *and* show jumping, horse trials need the skill and dedication of riders who are striving to become complete all-round horsemen and women. It says a lot for the younger generation that so many are taking up this arduous challenge each year.

It also says a lot for the selfless support they get from their parents, and other patrons, since the cost of a good horse likely to do well in eventing is soaring as the sport becomes more popular.

There were 41 official events in 1970, ten more than the previous year, and for the third year running there was a 30 per cent increase in the number of registered horses and starters, totalling well over 3,000.

The two big landmarks in the eventing season – split, in fact, into two seasons, in spring and autumn – were as usual, Bad-minton and Burghley.

In the former, inevitably, well known names dominated the leading positions, with Richard Meade and The Poacher in first place, Ireland's Captain Ronnie McMahon and San Carlos second, and Mary Gordon-Watson and Cornishman third. In the autumn Burghley was to some extent overshadowed by the world championship in Ireland which followed. Burghley was a most enjoyable event, three of Britain's best young riders carried off the honours: in first place Judy Bradwell, aged 21, and three times winner of the leading junior horse trials trophy, riding Don Camillo; second, Richard Walker, winner at Badminton the previous year, riding Upper Strata; and third, the young Scots rider David Goldie, with Rembrandt.

Yet it is well below the level of Badminton and Burghley where the most intensive growth is being seen in horse trials.

The lowering of the minimum age for competitors from 17 to 16 had a big effect on entries for horse trials. This had been done because Britain's team in the European Junior three-day championship had suffered through lack of experience over big courses up to the age of 17, through being ineligible for official Horse Trials.

With this problem in mind, the selectors chose a team for the 1970 Junior European championships which was strong in the ability to cross large, difficult courses.

Alas, the championship course last year, at Holstebro in Denmark, had a particularly easy cross country course. The dressage phase proved to be the most vital, and here the Germans were at an advantage. For the second time West Germany won the overall event, with France second and Great Britain third.

At home, the big increase in juniors and

Lorna Sutherland and Nicholas Nickleby at the last 34/35th obstacle of tree trunks, into water and jetty at The Three Day Trials, Badminton

49

Left; Mary Gordon-Watson and Cornishman V a superb combination across country
Above; Ireland's Captain Ronnie M. McMahon and San Carlos who came second at Badminton

other new event riders has been catered for by the highly successful Novice Championship, sponsored by the Midland Bank. Last year the same sponsor also provided a new Open Championship, the finals for this and the Novice Championship taking place at Wylye in the autumn.

The open event went, somewhat predictably, to Richard Meade and The Poacher, but they only just scraped home to victory by 1·33 points – the runner-up being an "outsider" from the North, Hazel Booth, who made a great impact by winning the Novice Championship on the same day.

Mary Gordon-Watson and Cornishman

She rode Mary Poppins II in the Open, and Deemster in the Novice championship. The Wylye cross country course had been built on the steep slopes of the Wiltshire downs with immense care and ingenuity by the hosts, Lord and Lady Hugh Russell.

It was the sort of course which lived up to the oft pronounced criteria of scaring the riders to death when they inspect it on foot, because of its awesome looking jumps and drops, yet being constructed so that it will not damage a horse even if it is not well ridden.

Jean Wathen's Ireland Monarch filled second place in the Novice event, with Judy Bradwell taking third and fourth places with Belle Grey and Justin Time.

Looking ahead, one of the biggest dangers in eventing is that an immense gap may appear between the standard of those at the very top, and the many at novice level who are struggling to train themselves *and* their horses.

It's been suggested there should be more two-day events to provide the transition from one-day to the tough three-day events. Some people feel dressage should be dropped from many one-day events, so that novices can concentrate most of their attention on the all-important cross country phase. Yet since most foreign competitors are especially strong on dressage, it would be a mistake to encourage our young riders to neglect it.

Apart from official horse trials, we are fortunate in Britain in having other opportunities for cross country riding – in the hunting field, and in hunter trials where there is no dressage element. Yet each year more countryside is lost to urbanisation.

Building good permanent event courses is expensive, but they are a wonderful invest-

Capt. R. McMahon and San Carlos

Lorna Sutherland and Gypsy Flame clearing the logs with plenty to spare

ment in the future, in providing experience for young riders.

So far Britain has done wonderfully through private patrons such as the Duke of Beaufort at Badminton, and others. But with the boom in the sport showing no signs of abating, perhaps some Government would think it worthwhile to give practical support to a growing sport in which Britain beats the world.

80

THE DAY BALLY WILL WILL . . . .
WOULDN'T

NEW STARS

Same old faces . . . it's a reaction one has heard as the leading show jumpers line up for their prizes at one of Britain's major shows.

It is true that successful show jumpers tend to be tenacious in remaining at the top. Self discipline and the will to win, plus sheer hard won experience, enable a select few to keep among the leaders in an increasingly competitive sport.

Their skill lies in staying among the winners on different horses, carefully bringing on new mounts to replace those currently doing well. A top show jumper constantly has to look ahead if he is to retain his position. The ability to keep on winning with new horses marks the real show jumping star.

Yet there must always be room for new stars if show jumping is to maintain its vitality and attraction. The names which came to the fore in the 1970 season were hardly completely new to show jumping. Success at the top comes only after seasons of hard work in a variety of contests.

The international progress made by Ann Moore, Betty Jennaway, Michael Saywell, Graham Fletcher and Raymond Howe is a splendid sign of the future. It is a fair bet that some, if not all, of these names will be consistently in British teams jumping abroad during the next decade. Always provided they can find the right horses, these young people will be an invaluable asset to British show jumping in the years ahead.

Michael Saywell, 27-years-old and from a Yorkshire farming family, had a superb first season with Trevor Banks's excellent bay gelding Hideaway. At 16·3 hands, and only seven years old, Hideaway is the sort of big, young horse who might well make an Olympic mount. He has tremendous scope and in his first full season jumping at international level he was wonderfully consistent.

Michael, a father of two, gets warm encouragement from his wife in his show jumping career, and she went to France with him – a well worth-while trip, since Michael and Hideaway won the Grand Prix at La Baule.

Michael told me something of his progress: "I don't know Hideaway's breeding exactly; I think he is out of a cart mare by a Cleveland stallion. But he is certainly a grand sort of a horse. He has a very stable temperament, and never jumps a bad round. If he hadn't made it in the show ring, he would have made a dependable hunter.

"I first rode him in the ring at the first

Ann Moore ▶

Michael Saywell and The Lodger

Hickstead meeting in 1970, and we finished second in the very first class we were in. We seemed to get on very well together from the start. He's a good ride, but he wanted a little more time spent on schooling him because he's only a youngster.

"Our Grand Prix at La Baule was ridden in terrible weather conditions. It was pouring with rain when we were jumping but it did not bother Hideaway at all. He was super; just went on jumping calmly as usual. We went clear in the first round and so were among the qualifiers for the second round, that was all those who had gone clear or had only four faults.

"In the second round we had to jump exactly the same course – but in reverse

With Carlawne in the Will's Castella Stakes

Mr. Whippy is Michael's partner here.

Ann Moore was in trouble at the eighth jump in the Will's Embassy Stakes

direction, starting at the finish and working our way round the fences to what had been the start of the first round.

"Hideaway was the only horse to go clear in this second round, so there was no jump-off or time penalties involved. I was very pleased, because being a young horse we do not want to jump Hideaway fast against the clock; we just want him to keep on producing careful clear rounds. It was a fair course at La Baule, but when the weather really broke up, the going was very heavy indeed. The open water, with no brush fence to mark take-off or landing, was an obstacle which upset a lot of horses. You could be faulted on either side of the water. Fortunately, Hideaway is very good over water and did not even look like putting a foot wrong.

"Jumping inside at the Royal International during the season was quite a big test for Hideaway, since being such a big horse he always goes better out of doors, but I have been very pleased with his performances in the indoor ring. He's a bold horse, but sensible as well, and with luck I think he should have a great future."

The successes of Ann Moore in 1970 came

86

Ann Moore and April Love

as no surprise. This blonde Warwickshire girl is short in stature, but extremely well endowed with skill and determination. With her bay gelding Psalm, and grey mare April Love, Ann was a most effective British representative. Psalm had been her mount when she won the European Junior Championship in 1968.

During their exciting 1970 season they won the major competition on the last day of the Madrid show in the spring and went on to contribute a string of further successes at home and abroad.

At La Baule in July she had a remarkably effective record in the classes which accompanied the Men's world championship. She tied with Alwin Schockemohle in the second main competition, and was unlucky to be beaten by about two seconds by Marcel Rozier of France in the speed event.

Ann was the leading money-winner at the La Baule show, apart from those taking part in the world championship. At Copenhagen Ann celebrated her 20th birthday by winning the Philips Cup event on the first day with Psalm, coming third in the same event

Graham Fletcher and The Whip during The Imperial Cup, at the Royal International Horse Show, Wembley

with April Love, who was formerly an Australian Olympic mount.

Ann was not selected to be one of Britain's two representatives in the Ladies' world championship at Copenhagen, but her attendance as reserve was praised as self-less and a bright future was predicted for her. If she can maintain such form she should almost certainly represent Britain in the next Ladies' world championship, and there were high hopes of her taking part in the next European championship.

At Rotterdam in the autumn Ann and Psalm were in the British team which came second to Germany in the Nations' Cup event – a British performance just good enough to secure the President's Cup for Britain on points throughout the season, having 36 points to Germany's total of 35. It was the third President's Cup for Britain since the championship started in 1965. Each country's six best results in Nations' Cup events during the season is counted in the season's total. The United States has twice won the cup, and the Germans once.

Much praise was heaped on 19-years-old Graham Fletcher, a farmer's son from Thirsk, Yorkshire, for his 1970 successes with Talk of the North and Buttevant Boy. Graham, cool in the ring, has the unflappability of a Yorkshireman outside the ring as well. He has the talent and the resolve to keep up Yorkshire's tradition of producing champion riders and horses. There is a long list from that county, but Harvey Smith's name will suffice!

Graham's home successes included winning the major event, the Wills Trophy, at the Bath and West Show when his rivals included David Broome, Harvey Smith, George Hobbs, and Alan Oliver. And at the Great Yorkshire Show he beat Broome and Smith to win the Blue Circle Badsworth Stakes. Graham had a marvellous Horse of the Year Show at the end of the season, his wins included a first and third in the Uniroyal International Championship of the Year. Buttevant Boy gained more points than any other horse and won Graham a new title – the Cortina Crown, which meant receiving a new Cortina car donated by Ford of Britain.

Graham has said that if he has not made the grade as a star by 1976 he will give up show jumping and concentrate on farming. Already as a 19-year-old he seemed to make the latter prospect even more remote.

From Billesdon, Leicester, Betty Jennaway comes to the big shows in the south, and crosses the Channel with great success. She is well established in the Midlands as a highly successful rider, and is now becoming better known internationally. Her 1970 string of victories included the Ansell's Brewery Supreme Championship at the Three Counties, the Clayton Dewandre Stakes at the Lincolnshire show, and the Norfolk Championship.

With her excellent eight-years-old brown gelding, No Reply, Betty rode in Britain's Nations Cup team in Lucerne when we finished second to the United States.

Also in the team at Lucerne was the 26-years-old Kent farmer Raymond Howe who had such a worth-while season with his greys Kalkallo Prince and Balmain. With Balmain he had one clear round, and four faults, in the Lucerne Nations Cup event. He

Betty Jennaway competing in the Queen Elizabeth II Cup

also rode in the British team at Rotterdam. His many home successes included winning the Talbot-Ponsonby Memorial event at the Royal International Horse Show against a strong field; Graham Fletcher was runner-up.

If they can maintain top form from their horses, these young riders will perhaps eventually become some of the "same old faces" always at the top. Consistency is the most important quality, and so far Graham Fletcher would be adjudged the most promising on these grounds. Both his principal mounts finished in the top ten prize winning horses of 1970.

Yet just to emphasise where the weight of prize money *still* goes year after year in Britain, here is the full 1970 list:

1st	Pitz Palu, ridden by	Alan Oliver
2nd	Mattie Brown	Harvey Smith
3rd	Sweep III	Alan Oliver
4th	Stroller	Marion Mould
5th	The Maverick	Alison Dawes
6th	Buttevant Boy	Graham Fletcher
7th	Ballywillwill	David Broome
8th	Spey Royal	Ted Edgar
9th	Beethoven	David Broome
10th	Talk of the North	Graham Fletcher

Raymond Howe and Kalkallo Prince winning the Talbot-Ponsonby Stakes at the Royal International Horse Show

1

2

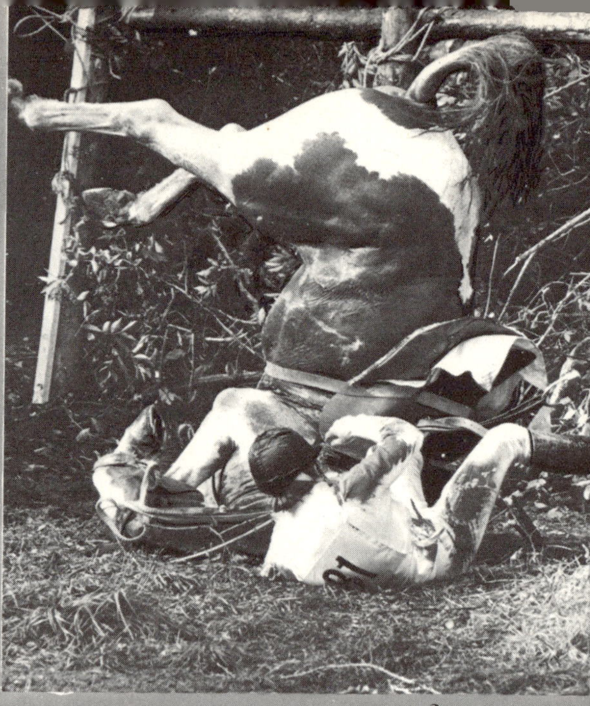

3

4

Lorna Sutherland and Popadom crash at fence twenty-nine during the
World Championship three-day event at Punchestown

MISADVENTURE

Anne Backhouse parts company from Cardinal II, during The John Player Trophy ▶

Looking back,
I suppose it could
have been worse!

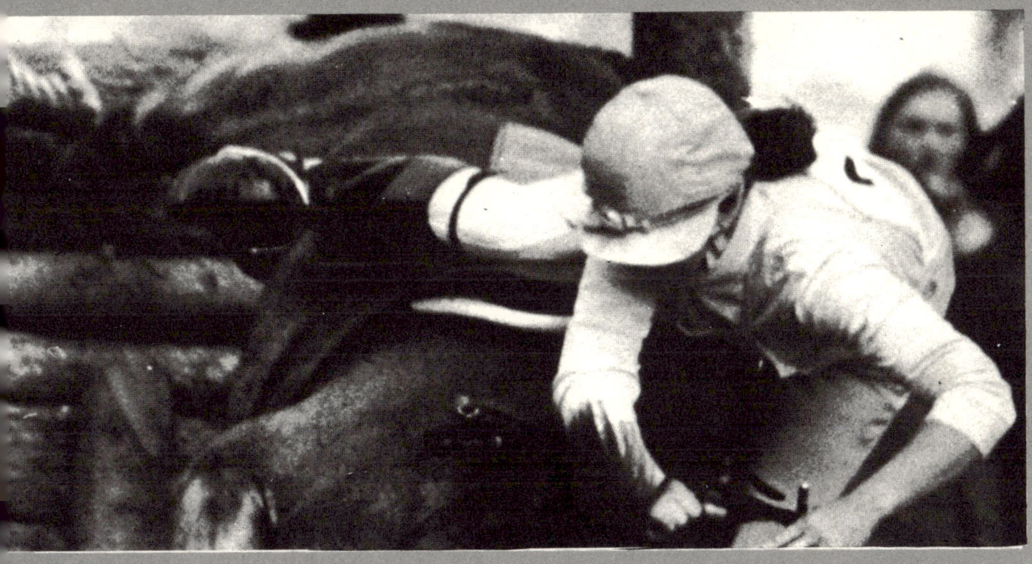